Meditations at the Table

Jim Waring

Happy memories

Jim

Tentmaker Publications
121 Hartshill Road
Stoke-on-Trent
Staffs.
ST4 7LU

ISBN: 1899003 56 8

Cover design: Anna Waring

Dedication

To the memory of my dear wife Martha, partner, companion and friend over many years, whose quiet wisdom was the inspiration for much of this philosophy.

Jim and I are members of the same local church and I am always grateful when Jim takes the table. His messages are characterised by real understanding of the Lord's supper, genuine usefulness for those of us gathered and a reverent joy which sets it all alight. I warmly commend these studies to you for devotional preparation in coming to the table of our Lord.

Graham Cheesman
Principal, Belfast Bible College

Introduction

This little anthology is a collection of short talks shared at the Table over a recent period of time. There was no intention of committing them to paper, but some friends had from time to time, been kind enough to express their appreciation, and suggested some form of written record. In particular, my friend Joe, without whose persistent pressure, I doubt if I would have put pen to paper.

Although I began the exercise with some reluctance, I have found the research and writing something of a pleasure, and I trust the end will justify the means. The contents, by their abbreviated nature, lay no claim to an exhaustive study, and any serious analysis might possibly disclose that they are somewhat of a devotional commentary on the various experiences of a long life, many of which I believe are common to most.

Those who know me best are aware of the high regard I have for what we sometimes refer to as the Sacrament of the Lord's Supper. I consider the essence of the Table to be pivotal in our worship and I trust that this motivation will be seen in what I have written.

Contents

John 19:25–27

"there stood by the cross, His mother…"

If Jesus is in the company, things are never as bad as they may seem. No matter how much hatred there is, there is also evidence of love. 'Where sin abounds, grace doth much more.' Sin may appear to be in the ascendancy. It can be crude, overwhelming, devastating as it was here on this terrible day. To mix the metaphors, the sky was alight with the flames of hell, while all the earth was shrouded in darkness. The evidence of evil was overwhelming. But grace can be found in little things of great value. The diamond may be small enough to be held in a ring on the little finger, but it may be more valuable than the shop from which it was bought!

Here, amidst all the trauma of the cross, all the scorn, hatred and humiliation, is the diamond of love. It is clearly seen in the life and death of the Man on the centre cross, but it also, as it always does, finds its reflection in some who take time to gaze upon it. Mary, suffering as no other, finds that love like her's brings healing as well as hurt. The love too, of that favoured disciple, finds expression in caring and giving. Real love always does. For God so loved, that He gave. It is the mark of all true lovers and we find God's pleasure when we practise it.

Luke 22:20

"This cup is the New Covenant…"

This is no ordinary meal. There is a satisfaction here that we find nowhere else. Well might it be described as new. Of course, there was a covenant in the blood of the Old Testament, but it was not His blood. What marvellous truth in Isaac Watts' encouraging hymn "not all the blood of beasts on Jewish altars slain". The old covenant allowed the Israelites to go free, but this covenant is sealed with a blood that goes on cleansing.

In the Old Covenant, those who obeyed it were promised God's help and guidance, but the people's sin was not finally dealt with. But here, in this Man's blood we have not only release from sin's eternal consequences, but power to defeat it in our daily lives.

The old was written in stone, cold and impersonal: the 'new' is written in our hearts with its capacity to respond in warmth.

The Apostle Paul was exultant in his language when contrasting the New Covenant with the Old. He was more qualified than most. The Old was his life—Royal tribe of Benjamin, Hebrew of the Hebrews, Pharisee of Pharisees. An impeccable history of conformity to the Law. Blameless, and a model inheritor of the Covenant, and what does he now say? In the light of what I have received in the New Covenant of Grace, I count it all loss.

Because it is His blood, He is the surety and guarantee of all that God has promised to do for us at Calvary. The same Lord who calls this the new covenant also declares "behold I make all things new".

Luke 23:34

"Father forgive them..."

Look at the background against which He prays this prayer. He has often prayed for His friends—we can understand that and practise it—but this time it is for His enemies and He had plenty of them: in fact more of them than friends. And don't we all, when our lives are such as they challenge the ways of others? We ought not to be surprised. How they hated Him!

Godliness has many mysteries about it, and this is one of them. There is great grace required in forgiveness. In fact the one begets the other. The Saviour was 'full of grace' and His forgiveness was magnanimous. As we have more grace in our lives and practise it, so the more forgiving we are. Stephen was a man of faith and grace when on his 'cross' of stones, rather than nails, he echoes the words of his Master "lay not this sin to their charge".

I have suggested in another place that effective forgiveness is meant to lead to reconciliation and as such requires the confession of the guilty one. However, there is a sense in which forgiveness is at its best and God-like when it is unsought and unrequited. A generosity of mind which looks benevolently upon those who have wronged us. 'May the mind of Christ my Saviour dwell in me from day to day'.

He loved us as enemies and made us His friends. When we forgive, we are in good company and, who knows, maybe in the mercy of God those we forgive will become our friends and His.

Luke 22:19, 20
1 Corinthians 11:24

"Broken for you"

When He says for you we can legitimately respond for me.

What a great comfort and encouragement that can be. It has always been so for those who recognise the presence of Jesus in their lives. There is something of divine possessiveness here. Paul says, "He loved me and gave Himself for me" and Peter declares, "He hath appeared unto me." This is one side of a glorious coin, which like any coin requires two sides to make it valid. On one side the world is our vision and parish, but on the reverse we are alone with Him. Almost a glorious selfishness! "Mine, mine, mine, I know Thou art mine."

This was for many, yes, and indeed in some sense for all, but although the many may say no and the all reject Him, it is still me for whom He died.

Everything He does is for you. It was so throughout His life: He lived for others. It was for you He planned to come, for you He came, and now for you this Table and all it represents. Let His parting words be our comfort: "I go to prepare a place for you and will come again for you."

Luke 22:19
1 Corinthians 11:24

"Do this in Remembrance of Me..."

There is something very personal here. The Passover was initiated to remember an event. And while it is true that the greatest of all events is remembered here at the Table, that is not what He asks. "Remember Me," He says. He is always pre-eminent. He is above and beyond everything He has created, and every institution and sacrament He has endorsed.

I don't think that those present on that solemn evening would ever forget Him, but it is good to be reminded. We all need that.

I'm sure your wife or husband will not forget your love, but it is nice to reinforce it with a present or a card, or indeed a sincere word of endearment. So at the Table we restate our love afresh and re-plight our troth as our memories are stirred. We don't easily forget who or what lies closest to our heart.

The cross is only effective because it involved Him. We echo the words of another who said, "we would see Jesus." May we see and know Him afresh as we remember.

Luke 22:14–15

'He fervently desires our presence'

"With desire have I desired to eat with you." Isn't it good to know when someone really wants us. We already know from His word and our experience that 'His presence makes the feast', but now to hear Him suggest that our presence makes it for Him, that our attendance here is a fulfilment of His desire! What an exciting and comforting thought that He longs to be in our company.

There are many sides to the Master, but here we have a singularly attractive one, that He longs after us. This is heart language. There is love and affection here and, in the context of this story, it was in spite of what He knew about the subsequent events of betrayal and desertion.

The prophet said, "there was nothing in Him that we should desire Him" and while we understand the context of that observation, it is not true of those of us who have come to know Him. He is the Lily of the Valley and Fairest of Ten Thousand.

This is His desire for us. May it awaken our love for Him and arouse our desire, as with all true lovers, to spend more time in His presence.

Mark 14:12–16

'Preparation'

The more important an event is, the more thorough is the need for preparation. "Put a tie on," says my wife. "But I'm only popping out for a paper," I reply. Ah, but if I was dressing for a wedding, what a difference that would make. So the end does, in some cases, justify the means.

I understand the Israelites could spend four days in preparing the Passover. Is there a greater occasion in all the church calendar than this Table spread before us?!

We need our heart and mind to be prepared. To have all our attention focused on the Saviour. When Jesus arrived the room was furnished and ready. We have expectations that here again this morning He will set our hearts aglow.

We encourage our young people to prepare themselves, to apply to their studies and work hard. We get nothing for nothing. And so it is here: even the grace that is free only comes to hearts prepared for it. He has prepared the Table for us, now we need Him to prepare us for the Table. Isn't it sad that sometimes we feel no blessing from our presence at the Table— maybe because we have not been prepared for it.

Soiled and unworthy we may feel, but He has a garment to clothe every guest. It covers every sin. 'Come for all things are now ready.'

Matthew 22:2–5, 8–10

'Come the meal is Ready'

What a privileged people we are! What a marvellous and spontaneous invite!

Consider the origin of the invitation. This is no friendly neighbour inviting us to a house-warming party. There is a Royal insignia emblazoned on this card.

But why us? What credentials do we have? You will note throughout Scripture how the Lord delights to entertain sinners. His invitations are wide-sweeping. There are none excluded who are willing to come. But not for us, surely? We are not properly dressed. Our garments are those of a sinner. But there are garments of purity available in the vestibule. We may dress in there and find a place at the table.

And what a banquet this is! A mere word of promise was all that was required to satisfy the wilderness people, or a few loaves and fishes with consecration to feed the multitude. But not here. This is costly food, part of heaven itself. This caused a division and separation of the Godhead. This impoverished God and robbed heaven. This is not just effort but surrender.

This table reflects His regard for us. His own flesh and blood—what more could be given? There is no entitlement—it is all of grace.

How could we possibly fail to respond to such love. May it find an echo in our hearts.

Mark 15:25

'They crucified Him.'

This is the ultimate of His many sorrows. It seems to me no surprise that many bow their heads and bend their knee in awesome reverence and worship in the presence of the Cross.

The Cross is eloquent in all it says. What a terrible thing sin must be, that it needed a Cross to deal with it. If we could but see our sin as God must have seen it no doubt we would treat it more seriously. Here, too, is some evidence of the value that God puts on the human soul. To Him it was worth all this to buy it back from bondage and restore it to its rightful owner.

The Cross is also the pattern for all our living. It is an act of spontaneous giving. An abandonment of self for the good of others. The more completely we forget ourselves and live for others, the more like Him we become. The Cross is a criticism of our selfishness and self-seeking.

Death on a cross covered a man's name and memory in shame. The Saviour lifted it to glory and made it an emblem of hope and promise whenever and wherever it is raised.

As sinners, we were by nature at enmity with God, and as such we were among the 'they' that crucified Him and we remain among their number if and when we allow the Cross to become non-effective in our lives. By the same token we are numbered with the faithful few around the Cross as we refuse to leave the scene and allow His dying love to make its indelible impression on our lives.

John 19:1-5

'Behold the Man'

Pilate, we can be sure, had tried many men, but never one like this. On three occasions in this short episode he declared that he could find no fault in Jesus and sought to release Him. His strong wish was to do it, but the will was not there.

Although these words were addressed to the mob, they might well have been spoken to us. Behold Him, gaze upon Him, give Him your attention.

Enduring mockery and shame, that we may have honour; thorns, that we might wear a crown of glory; a mocking robe, that we might be clothed in righteousness; reviled, hated, taunted, humiliated, yet, with a million angels on call, remains patient and long-suffering. He is a rebuke to our resentment and discontent and an encouragement to our ambition to be better.

He was a 'Man of Sorrows' who left joy in His wake. He thought well of every man who thought little of themselves. The joy that He had was in knowing that His sorrow was fruitful. And though, in a sense, the encouragement from His friends was less than it should, His eyes were on an eternity peopled with a multitude singing praises to His name.

This man is the God-man, holy, separate, yet a sacrificial Lamb bearing our sin, suffering for others. Was there ever a man such as He?

"This is My Blood"

The word of God, in another place, tells us that "the life is in the Blood".

Moses sprinkled blood on the people of Israel (Exodus 24:8) saying, "this is the blood of the covenant which the Lord has made with you." But a greater than Moses is here. The Saviour speaks as Moses never could: "this is My blood". The shadow has become real substance. He fulfils every prophesy and perfects every promise. The price has been paid and deliverance bought.

There was an old custom which nailed a cancelled bond on the wall of the debtor's home, for all the world to see that the debt was paid. So the blood on the door-posts told the angel of death that this house was secure.

As the nails draw blood on the Cross they also pierce the debt bond of our guilt and declare us free. He drained the cup of its bitterness, washed it in His blood, and filled it with sweet blessing for us.

Matthew 26:26–30

"He took bread…"

On that night of all nights He took bread, He blessed it, He broke it, He gave it.

Everything He does has significance and meaning. What more appropriate illustration for His body than bread. As bread is food to the body, so He is the nourishment for our souls.

Can't you see Him in the preparation of bread. The wheat is cut down, broken, crushed and baked in fire.

He broke the bread! In our pleasure at this table we must ever be aware of the cost. Broken, crushed, that He might become bread for our souls.

He gave it. This is more than an offer. There is something imperative, almost imploring, in the words 'here, take this'!

We receive this in grateful remembrance. It is not enough that He gives and offers Himself, we must reach out and take— so with all His blessings.

Exodus 12:13

"When I see the Blood..."

Of all the more obvious ways to release His people, God chooses blood. But what more relevant and effective means could there be? The Word of God states what medicine confirms, that "the life is in the blood". Get the blood right and we are well on the road to good health!

This first Passover night didn't just happen. There was much preparation in every household, for this was to be the most important thing that was ever to happen to this people. And so it was with the substance of what these table elements represent. All heaven was engaged in preparation for this. Slain, He was, from the foundation of time. This blood was flowing in eternity in preparation for Calvary.

It has always been God's intention to release and cleanse His people. And blood is the means by which He does it. To those early Israelites the blood only became effective as a means of escape when it was applied. They were obedient. They did what they were told to do. And so must we, if we are to be released from the penalty and power of sin.

> Let the water and the Blood
> From Thy wounded side which flowed
> Be of sin the double cure
> Save me from its guilt and power

Mark 15:38–47

"Those who stood by..."
Centurion

Men of authority recognise authority when they see it in another. One had a sick servant and sought the help of Jesus; another was Cornelius who feared God with all his house. This Officer at the Cross was impressed by what he saw.

No pomp or false majesty surrounded this King of the Jews— but there was real dignity in His death. In all his experience of superintending crucifixions, he had never seen a man die like this man. It persuaded him to acknowledge that Jesus was the Son of God—so unlike the Jews who claimed that "He made Himself to be the Son of God". It was written of him that he "glorified God". The believing heart always brings glory to God.

Here is a gospel for 'men' in the sense of strength and substance. In my work amongst young men in the Armed Forces, it was often their perception that what I was offering them was for 'old ladies and young girls', not for the macho life they found attractive!! Little did they know the courage it takes to pursue the godly life. But here was a man who was given eyes to see the stature of this man. Not given to sentimental tear-jerking but aware that this was no ordinary criminal. Your Saviour and mine is Man for all; for Centurions— and for 'old ladies and young girls'.

Here we have the Cross at work in a man's conviction and conversion. It still is the only means to peace with God.

Luke 22:7–16

"Passover"

This most prized and joyful of all the feasts. More like a birthday party, really, to celebrate and remember the day the nation was born again. A new start from Egypt.

But somehow this occasion was different. There was sadness and foreboding in the company. The release from Egypt was not enough. The question of continuing sin remained. And sin always mars and spoils. It turns rejoicing into mourning, joy into sadness, and so it does here. It brings a night of betrayal and desertion.

Isn't it good that He has destroyed the power of sin for ever. When the Cross and all it stands for is held high, 'devils fear and fly.' This Man of Sorrows brings joy to our hearts. His suffering brings healing and His death breathes life into our dead souls.

No occasion or event is ever impoverished by the presence of Jesus. Everything He touches is enhanced. He exalts the Passover to a Sacrament, for He did not come to destroy but to perfect and make substance of shadows.

Matthew 26:26

"Take eat..."

This is the most clearly seen of all the marvellous characteristics of the Master. He was always giving. He was never possessive of whatever it was He had. It began in eternity before the world began when He surrendered to the Father's plan to save the world. There is no commitment that is truly original, it all began in heaven. When one of old said, "here am I send me," it was an echo of the Lord's commitment given in eternity.

"My body"—no one can give more. "Greater love hath no man than this"—the life that was first offered to God is now offered to us. What glorious giving this is! And all of it prompted and born of love.

But He does say "TAKE"—If the giving is so willing and spontaneous, I will just as willingly take it. He gives Himself and His word declares that "with Him, He has given us all else". We take with gratitude and respond with ourselves. He gives Himself and we take with enthusiasm. How could we be anything other than richer in our soul.

Luke 23:44

"Darkness over all the earth"

All the mystery of this strange phenomenon is compounded by
the darkness. Something terribly black was happening here and
it would seem that even nature had suspended its normal
function to show sympathy with this classic drama.

But all this was as nothing when compared to the awful
darkness that enveloped His soul. Forsaken? He cried.
Mysteriously forsaken He was. Oh that we could appreciate the
awfulness of sin!

He was forsaken, that we might for ever be accompanied
for says He, "I will be with thee." He shrank from the 'cup'
that we drink joyfully in glad appreciation. Death need have
no bitterness for us: He drained it of its gall, and drew from it
the curse. Now we pass through only the 'shadow of death' on
our way to glory.

Wherever there is sin, there is darkness. And where sin
abounds as it did here the darkness is more dense than the
blackest of nights. The comprehensiveness of the darkness of
sin—'over all the earth'— serves to emphasise the glory of the
light that dispels it. No matter the darkness, wherever you find
the Light of the World, the dawn is about to break.

All the 'good' that we have and share is in consequence of
the 'evil' that befell Him.

Mark 15:27-37

"Numbered with the transgressors"

He ended His life the way He lived it: among people, transgressing people. He was at home in the presence of those who needed Him and those who transgress have a great need. On occasions it was 'tax gatherers and sinners'; another time, in the presence of an adulterous woman whose transgression demanded stoning; or again with a man shunned by the religious because of his illness. Should we not be eternally grateful, sinners that we are, that He is "numbered with transgressors"?

What a battle that was in the darkness of the cross during which no word was spoken. The sinless one, made to be a transgressor; how can we possibly understand that or identify with His suffering. No wonder He prayed, "let this cup pass from me" and, "Father, save me from this hour."

The suffering and humiliation is all His, that we might share in "the glory which He had with the Father before the world began".

John 19:25–30

Another faithful remnant

In spite of all the desertion at the cross there were still some whose loyalty held. Lovely to see that little group amongst all the antagonism. We are all encouraged by a friendly face in a threatening crowd. There are still those of us, relatively few in number maybe, who find comfort and encouragement around the Cross. It must still be a pleasure to Him to see the face of His friends at His table.

With one exception, at the cross they were all women! How strange: surely this is a place for strong men? But they have fled, only the weak remain. The heroes are not here—those who healed the sick and cast out devils—only the weak are here. The gospel often rebukes our estimate of strength and where to find it. Mary was a mother as mothers usually are. This was her boy who needs her support and she will not fail Him. John had just recently been close enough to Jesus to hear His heartbeat. Such a close proximity to the heart of the Saviour brings loving response and commitment, and the necessary strength to practise it. The nearer we are to Him the more help we are to others—"John, care for My mother."

John 1:29–36

"Behold the Lamb of God!"

Twice, John declares it, in case you haven't heard it the first time!

This is the preacher's first and only message; indeed none of us could do better than declare this to all our unbelieving friends. It was the theme of all John's ministry. I am not the Christ. I am not even Elijah or one of the prophets. I am just a voice with a message that you should look for another. If I am a light it is a 'star' that disappears in the light of the sun.

I can do nothing for your sin—but He can. He is the Lamb of God. Look to Him and upon Him. In their Wilderness dilemma, no Israelite mother, no matter how caring, could look on the serpent for her daughter's recovery. The healing was individual and personal.

I am a teacher, maybe a prophet, maybe many things, but I am not a 'Lamb', and certainly not the 'Lamb of God'. There is but one, go ye after Him.

So we look upon Him again in the emblems of bread and wine, and our hearts are warmed and our confessed sin forgiven.

Amongst other things that is a ministry of the Table.

Matthew 26:26–30

"I will not drink henceforth…"

This table is undoubtedly a place of remembrance. The feast is a memorial. But there is also tremendous hope here. He is not with us at the table anymore, as He said. That was indeed the Last Supper as we call it. Deep sorrow was evident but, as always, for those with understanding and ears to hear, there was a word of comfort: "we will sit together again."

You will note that the celebration in glory is the marriage supper 'of the Lamb'. Calvary is still the focus of all our eternal praise, for the cross is our reason for being there.

There is great paradox in His going. He leaves them that they might the more experience His presence. He has gone to prepare a place for us and, in the eternal hospitality of heaven, to set another table. That indeed is a day worth preparing ourselves for.

The freshness of this well-worn table is often to be found in the mind and response of those of us who sit around it.

Luke 23:26

"Simon of Cyrene on whom they laid the Cross"

Although it is true that Jesus bore the cross alone—He only could—there is a sense in which we share it. "That we might share in the fellowship of His suffering." What a privilege to 'carry His cross'. This is the work of every believer. But it is a cross of shame. Despised and rejected He was, Man of sorrows and acquainted with grief. This is an inevitable outcome of cross-carrying. If we take up His cross and become identified with Him, we will share the experiences of shame. He took up our sin, we take up His cross. But we must remember that it is His cross. That will help us when the scorn and the mockery and misunderstanding come—we do it for Him.

And there is glory in it. Who would ever have heard of Simon if he hadn't carried the cross. He has an honoured place on the record. And so will we if we bear it with honour.

The weight of the cross will win for us an eternal weight of glory.

Matthew 27:45–50

"My God, why hast Thou forsaken me?"

Was there ever suffering like this? He had much grief in His short life, but nothing like this. His friends had already deserted Him, but His own Father!? The One on Whom He could always count, was He not there? This was blackest midnight with a vengeance. None of us can enter this experience. We think that sometimes God has turned away from us, but He knew He had. What desolation. Nothing like this had ever happened before, nor could. He was not only the Priest but also the Lamb. Sin put Him there, but we have kept Him there.

But in all that darkness God was real and God was there. His reply was to lift the darkness and restore the sense of His presence. It is not in the nature of God to desert us. Obscured, maybe at times, by clouds of doubt and darkness, but always there. Just as the sun is beyond the clouds, He is as real behind the clouds as He is when the sky is clear. Of course we suffer agonies when we cannot see Him even though we know He is still there. What must the Saviour have felt when He knew the desertion was for real.

And He did it for us.

Luke 23:33–38

"Save Thyself" (1)

If You are what you claim to be, with all the power of the Almighty at your disposal, then come down from the cross. But He couldn't—well He could, but what would have been the outcome for us? He was committed to this mission of death by choice. Self-preservation is not consistent with love for others. Like a soldier in an important battle or a mother to save her child.

We come into the world to live; this Man came to die. When the crowd taunted Him with the cry of 'save Thyself', they were too late. He had already won the battle in the Garden on His knees and in the presence of His Father. All our struggles need to be fought there—it will stand us in good stead for the event itself, as it did for Him. The question of self-preservation was no longer an issue. There was no dissent on the Cross. All His thoughts were now for others and the Father's Glory.

The devotion of Jesus to the cross was complete. The stakes were high. The safety of all others and their eternal bliss and security were locked fast in the nails of the cross. And because He is the Good Shepherd, He gave His life for the sheep.

We are saved, and have become what we are because He refused to exercise His rights. His power and integrity were exercised, not in coming down from the cross, but in staying there against all the powers of hell and darkness to win our salvation.

When the work was finished, He allowed Himself to be lowered to the ground.

Luke 23:33–38

"Save Thyself" (2)

There were some things He couldn't do, bearing in mind His mission to the world. He had choices to make. Like a soldier in battle—Him or us. But Christ was devoted to death—"it is necessary for one to die."

His divinity only compounded His suffering. Because of who He was, He always knew the worst that was to befall Him. This was a part of His suffering we cannot share. Our lives are for the most part sunshine and showers—both experiences unpredictable and unknown in advance. There are occasions when we rest from our cross, but He never. Before He ever came, He took it up and carried it throughout His life. Holman Hunt depicts the young carpenter Jesus at the end of a tiring day at the bench, stretching His arms in relaxation. The rays of the sun cast a picture of a cross on the wall behind Him. Across the soul of even the boy Christ there looms the shadow of a cross. Well might He cry: "My soul is exceeding sorrowful."

Luke 2:30

"Mine eyes have seen They salvation"

We are often impressed by what we see, more perhaps than by
what we hear. We are in the age of teaching by visual aids. We
come back from where we've been, and we speak of what we've
seen.

We are, of course, influenced by our own particular interests.
We see what others don't, and miss what others see. It may be
the grandeur of the Alps or St Mark's in Venice or the paintings
of the masters in Florence or Antwerp. Or indeed that lovely
glen within easy travelling distance from where we live.

Someone has said that we should never neglect to look upon
a thing of beauty for it will colour our soul. Others have said:
"we would see Jesus." Simeon says: "I want no more, now that
I have seen Him."

Some old monks believed that if they looked intently upon
Christ on the cross, the marks of His wounds would appear on
them. Foolish, fantasy?—well maybe, but nonetheless true in
spirit. Looking intently upon Him does leave the mark of the
cross upon our lives.

Said another, who was after God's heart, "mine eyes are ever
toward the Lord."

John 13:20–27

Leaning on Jesus

We are not told the name of the one who leans on Jesus, yet there appears to be no doubt as to his identity. This last supper is probably the most portrayed of all the biblical incidents. Every artist seems to represent the apostle as gentle, affectionate, trusting and trustworthy. But wait; this man was a 'son of thunder' rebuked by Jesus for his intolerant vengeance. How he has mellowed in the company of Jesus.

Amidst all the demands that are made upon us in our personal, social and church life, there is a great need for comfort and consolation. We can often find it in our family and friends, but not always. The Apostle found the one sure dependable refuge. If the bosom of the Father was a place of perfection for Lazarus, we can be sure that there is no better place on earth. There is a suggestion of relaxation about 'leaning' which brings confidence, as distinct from 'clinging' which suggests desperation.

There is a time for leaning. There is much distress around us and often in us, and we need to lean on His sympathetic understanding. We need strength and we find it on His shoulder, but John finds the area of affection and love, and so may we. The Master wants us to rest upon Him and allow Him to bear our burdens. But He wants not only to bear our cares, He wants to feel us leaning upon Him, that the warmth which comes from Him will be our strength and encouragement and comfort.

Matthew 26:28

"For the remission of sins"

I like this record in Matthew. Neither Mark nor Luke mention the word 'sins'.

There are many things that distinguish us from each other. There is background and education. We differ in our appearance and attitudes. But this word 'sins' is common to us all, for all have sinned. But I'm glad that this Table is for sinners, as it was on that first night in the presence of the Saviour.

When I think about my sin, it would keep me from this Table and His pure presence. But when Jesus speaks of our sin, it is in the context of forgiveness. When we look upon sin, even our confessed sin, we may still grieve over it, but Jesus does not look upon our confessed sin. It is no more in existence, it is forgiven. If it is no longer in His memory, why should we allow it to clutter ours. He died to remit it. It is gone.

> 'My sin, O the bliss of this glorious thought,
> My sin, not in part, but the whole
> Is nailed to the Cross, and I bear it no more,
> Praise the Lord, it is well with my soul.'

Isaiah 53:6

"Sheep that have gone astray"

All we like sheep have gone astray, we have turned every one to his own way, and the Lord has laid on Him the iniquity of us all.

This is the common confession of the Prayer Book. Our sin is the one thing above all other than we have in common. But it is also special and peculiar to each of us: "every**one**." It is only when sin becomes individual and personal that it can be dealt with. It is an awareness of **my** sin, that might not necessarily be the sin of others. "To his own way" suggests our personal wrongdoing.

This is unreserved confession. There is no plea here of mitigation, no excuse is proffered. Our rebellion is broken, and our confession is complete.

But the cry of penitence gives way to song, for "the Lord has laid on Him the iniquity of us all". With all our waywardness and wilful disobedience, we are not abandoned. But oh, the cost! God will not break a bruised reed, but He was bruised and broken—bruised that we might be healed; broken that we might be made whole.

Hebrews 12:1–6

"'Who for the joy set before Him, endured…"

We often say, not always correctly, that 'the end justifies the means'. The more glorious the end, the more we are encouraged to endure the means. Even the fear of the dentist is eased by the thought of the removal of a painful tooth. Those awful last days of the Saviour were made bearable by the outcome. Nothing less than your salvation and mine, and hope for the world.

All the restrictions of pregnancy and the trauma of childbirth are relieved in the knowledge that "joy cometh in the morning". The face of pain is now wreathed in smiles. The baby is handed back to its mother. The happiness is complete when the offspring returns to its source. So we complete the Saviour's joy when we make His suffering effective and return to Him who is our source.

But what a tragedy when the birth is stillborn! All this for nothing. No cry of entry into the world. No response to love. He came unto His own and they did not receive Him. We are His own, those of us who have trusted Him, and He still comes to us in conviction and challenge, and He is sad when we do not respond. May we bring Him joy in all that we are and do.

"Good Tidings of Great Joy"

The gospel is always good news. No one was ever harmed by the gospel. No one ever sad in believing it. It is a tree with golden apples and silver bells. Even to brush against it causes a shower of good things to come our way.

It is good news of forgiveness to the sinner, as we all are. It is victory to those of us struggling with our weakness and temptation, comfort and encouragement to those of us who are fearful of the future and under stress in our lives.

What joy it has brought to this old world. Our orphanages and hospitals, relief and reform, all have their origin in men and women touched by the gospel and prompted to good works.

There is often a paradox when God is at work. The quietness of a Bethlehem hillside interrupted by a heavenly choir. In our mad world of haste there is a serenity in quietness, the noise of traffic is stilled by the carpet of snow. The awful foreboding silence of the Calvary day is transcended by the exultant cry of 'It is finished, into thy hands I commit My Spirit'. Bethlehem and Calvary, the beginning and end of an earthly life which has forever brought news of great joy.

The gospel has made us inheritors of much blessing. The angel spoke well when he declared it was good tidings of great joy. As we gaze upon the emblems of His dying love we are encouraged to take the baton from the angel and run to tell others that we bring good news.

Psalm 118

"Hallelujah"

The Passover feast provided the perfect occasion to sing this marvellous song of deliverance. But surely not on this occasion with the air filled with uncertainty and sad farewells to be said.

Hallelujah Psalm it may be, but I am sure there were few Hallelujahs that evening. But if they had only known! The release from sin, about to be enacted, would be infinitely greater than that from the bondage of Egypt.

The Lamb was in their presence and serving the meal. He would be slain, but not yet.

He could have erected a monument to His memory, but He chose the emblems that speak most eloquently of Him: His body, His blood.

Well may the Psalmist declare: "let all Israel say that His mercy endureth for ever." Well may our hearts echo with resounding confidence this Hallelujah of praise.

Here before us is the evidence that He is worthy. Everything that was asked of Him has been supremely accomplished for our salvation.

We come with gladness to worship Him. He is supremely worthy. He is King and reigns. Clothed with majesty, not wrapped in 'swaddling clothes'. Not in a manger, but seated on a throne as befits a King. The Apostle John in his Revelation during his island isolation waxes eloquent in his Hallelujah Doxologies to Him who sits upon the throne. 'Grace and peace from our Lord Jesus Christ—ruler of the kings of the earth. To Him Who loves us and has freed us from our sins—to Him be the glory and power for ever and ever'. There is no other response than 'Hallelujah'!

Matthew 26:28

"My blood… shed for many"

The number around the Table may be small, but the Table itself has great width and vision. On some occasions it was 'for you', at other times 'for me', but here is the Saviour with an open heart. Just as it is encouraging for us to feel the touch of the Saviour upon our individual lives, so we are reminded here that we are part of a greater company.

At the Table we join with our friends down the road and many, many others throughout the world whom we do not know and have never met. All part of the 'many' for whom His blood was shed. The Table is a great unifying force, as our differences are submerged in the blood. We are not only in unity with Him, but also with all those who acknowledge Him as Lord.

But this 'many' is so comprehensive—His blood was shed for our unconverted family and friends, …and for those who are less than friendly.

We are instruments in sharing His grace with others. As we receive His grace again at the Table, we are reminded that this same blood was shed for many.

1 Corinthians 10:16

"The Cup of Blessing which we bless"

With all the foreboding and solemnity of that awful evening, the Apostle calls upon us to raise our cup in thanksgiving. Whatever the disciples might have felt around the table, and it is fair to assume that there was no spirit of praise, there was an anticipation of victory in the sad heart of the Master. He gave thanks; He sang! We don't give thanks for catastrophe, and we don't sing in the face of adversity.

This is a prelude, a foretaste of that Song of the Lamb, which we will sing with joy around another Table far more glorious than this.

Let's come to the Table this morning with joy in our heart. We have every reason to look upon this cup with thanksgiving. It is the basis of all our hope and we speak well of Him and sing praise to His name for all that he has done for us. This is a cup of blessing because it is the "communion of His blood" and with it, taken in confession, we may feel clean again.

I Corinthians 11:28

"Let a man examine himself"

No one can share the Table meaningfully without self-examination. The Apostle says in another place, "Prove yourself, know that Christ is in you." If you have been born again of the Spirit of God, then be sure that Christ is in you. And if Christ is dwelling in your life, you are fully qualified to be here. You may feel yourself to be the weakest of Christians, you may indeed be the weakest of Christians, but that has no bearing whatever on your entitlement to be in this company. You are a child of God and, as with all children, you have a right to sit at your Father's table.

So we take our self-examination a stage further, seeking whatever in our lives brings grief to the Lord. This Table represents all that Christ did to take away our sin and it is a good place to reflect upon our need for confession and forgiveness. Do not be embarrassed to acknowledge your sins. We don't cast stones at the Table because we all live in glasshouses.

It was conviction and confession that brought us to the Saviour and the same will bring blessing and healing at the Table.

Numbers 21:5–9 (John 3:14)

Brazen Serpent

The Cross is not just a New Testament concept, it is deeply embedded in all God's dealings with men. There is a Cross throughout the Old Testament. It is symbolic in all God's provision for His people. It has always been His intention that a cross would be the instrument in our salvation. In our reading we have the pattern of behaviour that is often repeated in the Old Testament: disobedience, judgement, repentance, deliverance and healing.

The cure for all our ills can only come from God's provision, and in God's way.

The serpent was God's idea, not that of Moses or the people, and like all God's provision was sufficient. It always is. It still is. This way of the Cross is His way and we are privileged recipients. The God of Calvary is the God of Numbers and, indeed, of Genesis.

Imagine, a Cross! Whatever was God thinking about to initiate such a demeaning and humiliating way of release? No wonder wise and learned people consider it to be foolish; but to those of us who believe it, it is the saving power of God.

John 2:7-8

Co-workers with Christ
"Fill the pots with water... pour out now"

Of course He could have provided wine without the help of others. But He chose not to. This is His norm. He invites us to share in His marvellous works of grace, not because He needs to, but because He wants to.

Some may say we cannot do much, but neither could the servants in this crisis at the wedding feast. Often all He asks for is water. Surely that is not outside our reach. No matter how insipid our lives may be, they can sparkle like the best wine when touched by the Master. Everything He touches is improved. Every company is enhanced by His presence. Here is the pattern for our relationship with others.

The blessing is not in the gift, but what He does with it. It was only a branch in the hand of Moses, but what a wonder when it struck the rock. All the boy had was his lunch, but what provision! The Table is all divine, but are all priests in sharing its message of forgiveness and healing.

If our desire is to please Him, there is no such thing as ineffective service. There is no vain labour when we do it to please the Lord.

Mark 11:7–11

King... but not yet

This Palm Sunday could have been His day. He had claimed to be King, now He could be. The occasion was ripe and the crowds ready to crown Him. They had just seen that stunning miracle that brought Lazarus from the grave. So out came the palm branches and garments and the hills echoed to Hosannas.

But, as ever, they misunderstood the signs. Could they not see that with Him, the Prince of Peace, there was no evidence of triumphalism? All this pageantry was a prelude and not an end in itself. It must not supersede the event it heralds, whether it be a Coronation, or the Opening of Parliament or the beginning of the Olympics. This celebration was to lead to Passion and a Cross, and the tree was to be no Palm. The road to glory is not Olivet to Jerusalem with its palms, but Gethsemene to Calvary with blood, sweat and tears. Cries of Hosanna become those of Crucify.

Real glory only comes through suffering and self-denial. The Lord finds glory in what these emblems of the Table represent. A broken body and shed blood. "My Son in whom I am well-pleased" is the final accolade of approval.

Hebrews 2:10

"Made perfect through suffering"

Which of us is without suffering of one kind or another. Much of it beyond treatment by medication. There is a sense of isolation and loneliness, family hurt, disappointment with friends who have been less than dependable. Is it not also true that we often find most help from those who have themselves suffered?

But was not our Lord already perfect? Son and co-equal of an eternally perfect God. Lamb without blemish. Perfect already, yet now made perfect. Perfect in holiness, that He might make us holy. But now in a weakness He had never known, His identity with us is complete. It is a strange paradox that suffering which weakens and kills can perfect that better part of us.

With all the disadvantage that suffering brings, and who of us wants to suffer, might it not be a learning process that fits us for a service that God wants us to give to others?

Suffering can soften our spirit and make us more sensitive to the hurt in others. That is a process of re-action which can add to our perfection.

Matthew 26:36–46

"He began to be sorrowful"

He "began…"! Surely not? Was not His whole life one of sorrow? There were tears over Jerusalem and at the tomb of Lazarus. But somehow this sorrow of Gethsemene is different. It is of another dimension.

We can identify with Him as He cries over Jerusalem, or weeps at the grave of His dear friend, or mourns with the distraught mother whose dead son is being borne out of the city. But this sorrow of the garden is beyond our understanding. It belongs to His God nature. It underlines the awful impending prospect of abandonment and separation from His Father. Even His spirit was stooping with pressure. "My soul is exceeding sorrowful." He had never felt like this before, nor indeed spoken like this before.

This is what approaching Calvary did to the Saviour. It was the beginning of a sorrow never known by any other, nor could be. This Table is steeped in sorrow. A man of sorrows, He was, and fully acquainted with grief. And it was all for us and our salvation. May the awareness warm our hearts to His love.

Luke 24:13–27

Easter Joy

Whatever this glad day might mean to us, or however happy our hearts may be, we are never very far away from this Table. But need we spoil our Easter joy by allowing our hearts to be sad? Maybe not, providing we understand that we can't have one without the other. There is a glow around the tomb on Easter day, but it wasn't always there. You cannot have a resurrection of a death that never was. It takes two sides on any coin to make it valid.

We sometimes say the joyful first cry of a baby cancels out the trauma of labour, but like most of our assertions it is less than the whole truth. The new-born baby owes everything to the long and painful frustrations of months.

But He is alive this morning, and this makes credible His claim "able to save to the uttermost... because He ever liveth" (Hebrews 7:25). No dead priest, no matter how great, can plead our cause in heaven. Dead we were in our sins, but now we are alive in Him. "Because I live you shall live also."

We meet in the sadness of the Table with the joy and assurance of Easter in our hearts. What a glorious paradox here spread before us.

Hebrews 4:14–16

There is Mercy and Grace here
"…that we may obtain mercy and find grace to help in time of need."

If it is "mercy and grace" that we need, then every moment of our lives is an hour of need. And if we are looking for them, what better place to find them than at the Table. These elements concentrate our mind on Him who is the source of all supply—of all mercy and all grace.

We share a common affliction around the Table. We are in the near presence of One Whom we have grievously offended at times by our wilful disobedience and we need mercy else we perish. Our only right to be here is that we have been shown mercy, and we need to return often for more of it. Some of us are more committed. Some are nearer to Christ-likeness in our daily living than others. But none of us stands without need of mercy.

As for grace, how we need that. How can we possibly cope with life's demands without help. Our circumstances are sometimes more than we can bear. Family and friends may be well-meaning but we may need more. We need grace to suffer if we are not to be cured, grace to deal with misunderstanding and criticism when our motives are pure.

This without question is a Table of mercy and grace. We will find here all that we need.

Hebrews 7:25

"Able to save to the uttermost"

We speak here of the incomparable Christ. There has never been anyone with His ability to meet our need, nor can there ever be. There is no one who cannot be reached by what He has done.

Whether converted or unconverted, this work is for all of us. But there are essential pre-conditions before His saving and forgiving and transforming work can be effective. We will only look for a Saviour and Priest if we are aware of our personal sin and need. Without this we will not seek Him. If we become complacent and self-satisfied we are more likely to see Him as, maybe, a teacher or as a good, even perfect, example to follow.

But this Table will not mean as much as it should, if we are not conscious of our sin. For the most part we are respectable, law-abiding and well-intentioned, and sin may not appear to be all that active in our lives. But I tell you this, on the authority of God's word and in the light of experience, that sin, like sediment at the bottom of a glass, lies settled at the root of our lives and, when disturbed and activated, will muddy the waters of our walk with Christ and mar our testimony before others. We are all and always within His capacity to save.

Matthew 28:17–29

"Lo, I am <u>with you</u> alway"

One of the words spoken on that quiet and sorrowful night was for you. "My Body broken for you." "My blood shed for you." This Table and all that it represents was for you. But, as with everything, the Saviour's work is all embracing and He also says "with you".

When He says for you, it can only be proved to be true when we exercise faith to believe it. When we were first told that this was for you, I doubt if we really believed it. But when we did, what a change it made to our life. Forgiven and at peace in our conscience before God. Now the same dependable Jesus says, "I will be with you." There are no doubt times when this promise is difficult to believe. Our circumstances do not suggest His presence, else how could we possibly be in this position?

Just as we needed faith to believe in the saving message of the Table, so we need to believe that He will never leave us. A cloud may overshadow us, and sometimes it does, but faith will allow us to rise like a plane above the clouds of doubt and adversity to see that, whatever the circumstances, the sun always shines.

Hebrews 9:26

Once, only

When the High Priest was called upon to deal with sin, his own as well as that of others, he was required to return each year to repeat his offering. Whatever that act did, it did not take away the sin. Sins were no doubt remembered and confessed, but they remained to raise their ugly head, to be dealt with again another year. The blood he used in the offering was that of bulls and goats. It was not his own, and if it had been, it would have been no more effective.

But the work of Christ on the Cross needs no repetition—"in that He died, He died unto sin once." Everything He does is perfect, so it never needs to be repeated. When we are required to try again, it usually means we have failed. We re-sit our exams, we re-take our driving test. There is little we do that could not be improved with repetition. Not so with the Lord Jesus. He cemented His claim to have done all that the Father required of Him with that marvellously conclusive cry on the Cross: "It is finished." What a glorious Great High Priest He is!

Hebrews 7:24–28

Incomparable Priest

There are priests, as we all are, with direct access to Heaven, and there have been High Priests with special appointment and favour, but the Word of God calls the Son "Great". We know Him to be the greatest. After the order of Melchizedek. That mysterious priestly king whom Abraham met and whose characteristics were that he had no beginning and no end.

We are in good hands when our case is handled in heaven by the Great High Priest. When He speaks with God on our behalf, He is listened to with favour for He is the Father's favourite Son. In any prayer we offer, we do well to plead His name, for only that will ensure that our prayer is heard.

Just as there is no limit to His power to save—to the uttermost—so there is no limit to His priestly office. Other good priests have their tombs, but this Priest's is empty. "He ever liveth" to plead our cause before the Father. No sons of Aaron, with all their admirable qualities of priesthood, can boast of a continuing priesthood beyond the grave. Incomparable He was and is.

Hebrews 1:4–8

"So much better than the angels"

Even if the Bible did not tell us so, we know that there are degrees of creation. From insects, invisible to the human eye, through the lower order of animal life, to the creation of man with his authority over the rest, and beyond man into the realm of the spirit world we have angels. We need never doubt their existence for they are well documented—from the gate of lost paradise to the gates of the new Jerusalem of paradise regained; they sang at Bethlehem, fed Elijah and led Peter out of jail. The very law was ordained of angels (Acts 7:53). The Jews held the Law in the highest esteem, but the gospel is greater. Angels were messengers, He is the message.

Uncreated, He ever was. By Him were all things created. God made Him the inheritor of all that He has and is, and we share it with Him. Untainted with sin, and of the very nature of God, only He could have done what He came to do. God gave His highest and best and through Him, has made us sons too. No angel could take away our sin. Made "a little lower than the angels" in His condescension, but now "crowned with glory and honour" beyond them. And He is your Saviour and friend—and mine too.

Hebrews 9:14

"How much more..."

Speaking of what Christ has done, this is a question which cannot be answered. If we are asked, 'Is it more?,' then the answer is 'Yes'. Is it more valuable? Yes. Is it 'much more'? Yes. But 'how much more' is a question incapable of answering. It is immeasurable because there is no comparison. One is perfect, the other imperfect. Imperfect, because it (tabernacle) could not be otherwise, for it is "made with hands". It belongs to earth, the other made in heaven. Because man is involved the work is tainted. Even the High Priest, with all the virtue of his high office, was not allowed on the Day of Atonement to enter the Holy place to plead for the people, until he had made atonement for his own sin.

We ask rhetorical questions when we wish to make a point rather than seek an answer, and this is one such.

We just allow ourselves to be lost in meditating upon the wonder of what is, and is to be, compared to that which was.

'How much more?' Only God Himself can measure the answer to that. We are the benefactors.

Psalm 40:6

"Sacrifice and offering Thou would'st not"

David, as much as any, had seen the constant repetition of sacrifice. Day after day, year after year, and still the people were as sinful as ever. David could see, as could all other godly men, that none of it could take way sin. In another place, the Psalmist declares, 'I delight to do Thy will O Lord, Thy law is written deep and clear in my heart.' This commitment and willingness to obey His word and will, will please God more than any sacrifice we may claim to make.

When the Psalmist speaks here of his ear being opened (pierced), he is harking back to the practice (Exodus 21) of the freed slave who chooses rather to stay with his master. The opened ear was a declaration of the servant's commitment to "serve him for ever". That commitment is still more meaningful than any sacrifice. When salvation touches us our ear is opened to His every call. We hear Him now, where we didn't before. He calls us to obedience rather than sacrifice. Sacrifice, whatever it was in the Old Testament, is not now for us. His broken body is the only sacrifice that matters, for it does what no other could ever do: it takes away our sin.

Hebrews 8:10–13

A New Covenant
"I will be to them a God and they shall be to Me a people."

This is not just a better covenant than the one before. It is a completely different one. The idea of covenant is pretty clear to most of us. It is an agreement between two parties. The one agrees to do certain things if the other will do certain other things. This in some measure was the essence of the Old Covenant. There was a great big 'if' in every clause. While the people of Israel remained faithful God responded. Prosperity was conditional on obedience. There was at least one occasion when God said, "you are not My people" (Hosea 1). But this New Covenant is steeped in grace and perpetual forgiveness. In some ways, it is so one-sided as not to be a covenant in the way we know. Notwithstanding our unfaithfulness, He remains faithful. God sees in Jesus all the demands made of man to fulfil the human side of the contract. We could never fulfil our side of the covenant any more than Israel. But the emblems of the Table tell us that He has done it on our behalf. The Covenant, if that is what it is, is indissoluble, independent of our failure, and completely dependent upon His eternal unfailing faithfulness and grace. Well may we treasure it.

Hebrews 9:15–17

Inheritance

The Testament is not effective until the death of the Testator.

Your inheritance and mine of forgiveness and security was conceived in eternity. The first and last will and testament of the Almighty had your name and mine among the list of benefactors.

For the Christian, all real blessing comes in God's own time. This is a lesson we find difficult to learn. We are by nature impatient and find waiting hard to bear. There is a classic story in the New Testament to remind us of the dire consequences of insisting on our own timetable. The young man who could not wait for his inheritance ended up in all kinds of trouble. It pleases God when we wait with patience for Him to do in us and with us what he purposes. When we consider the awful things that happened in the Old Testament we might rightly guess that the Lord Jesus was tempted to come earlier than He did to set things right. But He didn't. Everything He does is in "the fullness of time". And when He did come, He sealed and secured our inheritance. The Table bears record that the Testator has died. The will has been read and we have entered into our inheritance of forgiveness and peace. And this, in some ways, is a down payment of something even greater.

Revelation 14:1

A Lamb on Mount Zion
"And I looked, and lo, a Lamb stood on Mount Zion."

John was very privileged in seeing into Heaven, and we too are privileged that he describes, as best he can, what he saw. "Lo, a Lamb," not just a glance or a look, but "Behold". Stop in your tracks, gaze, think upon it, give it your attention. It could have been a King in regal colour, or a Being of infinite glory and grandeur. But no, a Lamb! And why not indeed. Everything we are and have we owe to the Lamb. No wonder He is the centrepiece of Heaven. John was oblivious to all else when his gaze was drawn to the Lamb, and no doubt there were many other wondrous sights. This was God's instrument in taking way his sin; and he was forever indebted. He was glad in his lonely exile and free in his prison. We look not merely to the Table, but into Heaven to gaze upon the Lamb. He it is who has redeemed us. No kingly autocrat, no sublime angel, but a Lamb.

When we see Heaven we see the Lamb and, conversely, when we gaze upon the Lamb we are in Heaven. Christ and Heaven are inseparable. If to be in Heaven is to be with Christ, then to be with Christ is to be in Heaven.

Luke 22:19

Remembrance

Memory is a strange faculty. It is not nearly as strong as
forgetfulness. We know from personal experience that it is much
easier to forget than to remember. We don't need to make a
conscious effort to forget, but we need to work at remembrance.
It is fashionable to-day 'to move on' as we call it, to bury the
past, to draw a line in the sand, and to start with a clean page.
But life is not like that. There is a continuity in it for to-day is
in some respects a consequence of yesterday. There is no present
without a past. That is the significance of the table. We are
what we are because of what the Saviour did 2000 years ago.
Free from the bondage and penalty of sin.

But why the Table? When Jesus said, "remember me,"
wasn't that enough? Of course we know it isn't. We are so
forgetful; that's why we keep diaries. So our attention is focused
with a visual reminder. It is important to be reminded to
remember. It is even more important not to allow the motions
to replace the motive. We concentrate on the body and not the
bread and on the blood and not the wine.

But remembrance is meant to be positive. It demands a
positive response. When the love of our live asks, "Did you
remember my birthday," we know she doesn't mean the date,
it is the gift of an affectionate card or a meaningful present, or
both, which is the appropriate response.

Ephesians 2:4, 5

Such Love

'Such' is a somewhat neutral, colourless word and yet as a descriptive adjective it has the emphasis of a superlative—such irony, such pleasure, such cruelty. It is entirely appropriate in the context of the love God has for us. How could He possibly love someone who in every way is his enemy? From our birth we have grieved him with our rebellion. He knew not only what we were but how we would become worse, and yet He loved us! He is undaunted by our sin notwithstanding the hurt it has caused Him. He foresaw all our failings and broken promises and yet he persevered with us because He loved us. If He loved us in our willing sin and rebellion while unregenerate, we may be sure He will still love us in our acknowledged daily backsliding.

We find it difficult to understand such love which is not determined by our nature and mood. Although we cannot comprehend it, it is a gift that we may apprehend.

This love represents total giving. God tells us when He gave Jesus, He gave all. The measure of the gift reflects what He thinks of us. We do not give token gifts or trinkets to those we really love. We may send a card to our friends and acquaintances at Christmas, but it could well be a computer or tricycle to our children. There are no trinkets with God. All His gifts are "Royal Doulton". Only the best—such is His love.

2 Corinthians 8:9

Grace!

What a lovely word this is! There is no entitlement to grace: it is a gift bestowed. We are familiar with 'grace and favour homes'. They are enjoyed by some at the behest of the Sovereign or the Government. There is no contract, no payment except in so far as when the status of the occupant goes, the tenancy is surrendered. The grace and favour shown to us is as permanent and secure as our salvation. Grace is the sole prerogative of God. He dispenses it with extravagant generosity because its supply is boundless. Grace is only given to those who are deserving of judgement.

We can give God much. Love and talents and time, but never grace. It is the epitome of his character. He was eternally rich. Poverty was unknown in his environment. While he remained rich and we poor, there could be no reconciling contact. Everything he did was to enrich and ennoble us. Having planned it all in eternity He set about implementing our reconciliation. He came down from where He was that we may rise to where He is. He gave, that we might take; was stripped that we might be clothed; soiled that we might be clean. All of it 'for our sakes' say the scriptures. 'Gave up everything for me' says the hymn-writer. The Word of God, as with God Himself, is lush with grace. Well might Newton call it "amazing".

Primacy of Grace

Isn't Grace a marvellous thing? It never ceases to amaze me how God envelopes His judgements in grace. The Table is a classic example. There is judgement written all over it. There is brokenness in the bread, the blood of life is spilt. There is a pall of death hanging over it. Yet in some ways what He has done on the Cross should be no surprise when we consider the history of His dealings with us.

It is the very essence of God's nature to treat us with generosity. It is said that God "hallows the unhallowed". He is forever reminding us that there is nothing and no one outside His love. Take the young mother for example. How He loved mothers! He selects a pregnant teenager, unmarried and unhallowed and He confirms her in the blood line of His redemptive plan. Who else could have thought of such a scheme and such an instrument. Chosen and blessed among women, yet acknowledging that God was her Saviour. We salute her memory as we do all mothers, but we share her confession of a need for a Saviour. All of it is grace indeed, to her and us, and yet, as the women (yes, women again) poured their gifts of perfume to quench the stench of death, so He pours His grace upon the emblems and they become our rainbow of hope.

What kind of man is this, to cover even His 'legitimate' judgements with grace!?

What manner of love is this

In a sense this is more a question that a statement. It invites an answer, if we can find one that does justice to the question. God "did not spare His only Son"; but did not others before and since do the same? We often draw analogies from Scripture to illustrate the attributes of God, but significant and helpful as they are, they remain inadequate. If we think of the greatest example of loyalty and obedience to God, Abraham must be high on the list. But do remember there was a substitute for Isaac in the thicket, there was none for this man. God can only forgive sin on the strength of Christ's death. He was tried and found guilty for our sin—unknown as it was to those who convicted Him. For us now there is no condemnation. It is the law of heaven, as it is a law of ours, that you cannot be tried twice for the same offence. Who or what can now condemn us? God, who is the final authority when it comes to judgement and forgiveness, has dealt with our sin in His own way. He who has every right to charge and condemn us, has rather chosen to forgive us. It is such that 'neither tongue nor pen can show'. We simply bask in it, in grateful remembrance of all He has done for us.

This is Worship

The Table is more than an act of remembrance; it is an act of Worship. Remembrance itself can be a passive thing, but worship can give expression to its significance. The Lamb has always invoked adoration. We are told that the redeemed in glory "worship the Lamb that was slain!" What a glorious activity to anticipate. A blissful exercise 'uninhibited' by the restraints of sin.

There are many things that are a means to an end, but worship, primarily, is not one of them. We do not come to worship that we might obtain blessing. The sole motivation for worship is that He is worthy. We worship Him for what He is and what He has done. We dare not lay claim to blessing, for with all our repeated cleansing at the Table and elsewhere, we remain sinners and an offence to God in its practice. And yet, and yet, for all that the Psalmist says, although we cannot flee from His Judgement, neither can we escape His grace. This Table of worship is a place of grace. In our confession, the Lord gives an awareness of His presence, and there is no greater blessing than that. His presence will make any feast.

So, true worship, an end in itself, is non the less pregnant with blessing—and nowhere more so than at the Table

Mark 14:32

"My soul is exceeding sorrowful"

The Scriptures don't often speak of the soul of the Saviour. When He Himself speaks of it, we must surely take note of it. This Gethsemane experience appears to be something quite different from anything before. His humanity seems to go beyond His divinity. Although He knew from the beginning that this moment would come, when it came it was almost too traumatic to bear and He was "distressed and troubled" (v 33).

Jesus shared much of His life with His friends, but some of His experiences were so personal that He sought only the company of a few. The pattern followed on that fateful night was typical of many others. Away from the crowd He had a meal with the twelve, then into the garden with the intimate three, and then, as the pressure mounted, He sought solace in the presence of His Father who understood Him most perfectly.

The suffering here is so great that His humanity asks for something He cannot have. "All things are possible"—not this. He, more than anyone, knew that it was absolutely necessary "that one should die". This was suffering beyond the intensity of nails. This 'soul' was the God-part in grief. There are wounds that do not draw blood; that would come later.

Sometimes in pressure, our humanity asks amiss. We look for an alternative to God's way. But the bottom line is submission, as it was for Him, then grace to bear is available to us, as again, it was for Him.

Love Expressed

On this Valentine Day, we are met in the presence of the greatest love of all time. You know my respect for the dignity of the Table and I would not trivialise it by comparing it with something that is not on the same plane. There is no Valentine like the Table. This is the greatest expression of any man's love. To many young men the object of their love might be Sarah for a while, then maybe Mary, and possibly others, but not here at the Table. There is an eternity in this commitment, surpassing even the best and longest of loving commitments.

We are familiar with the words of the marriage ceremony "till death us do part" reminding us of the fragility of the human relationship, but there is a principle here which is equally valid in our union with God. No death, nor parting. The eternal nature of our life in Christ ensures no ending and therefore no parting. Everything we have in Christ is always that much more than even the best we have in this life.

For the most part we love those we find attractive. But never with Christ. Knowing all about us, He yet loves us and, despite our crass failure, He finds no reason to repent of His love.

There is no 'guess who' at the bottom of this Valentine. His name is written all over it. There is really no reason for it, other than He is just a loving Lord.

"To obey is better than sacrifice"

There were many events in the life of our Lord which helped shape the course of history but none so significant as the Cross. Not even the coming of the Messiah was as important as His death. For having come into the world, He still could have opted out of His mission in His soul-struggle in the garden.

In an informed national discussion of history's sea-changing events, someone commented that the Cross was the biggest thing that ever happened—and it was. Its consequences were history-changing as well as life-changing. Our destiny is determined by our response to what happened at Calvary more than to any other of the demands that heaven makes on us.

And yet it is not so much the Cross as the obedience which brought it about. When, in that agonising struggle in the garden, He declared, "Not My will..." the Cross was assured. To obey is always better than sacrifice for all real sacrifice is a consequence of obedience. God always rewards obedience with blessing. Obedience may have put Him on the Cross, but it was God who raised Him from the dead and blessed Him with a Church family greater than can be numbered. The joy that was set before Him was an inheritance He counted worthy of the Cross: the first fruits of all who believe.

If obedience is the hallmark of our Christian life, then be assured of God's approval and blessing.

Beyond Understanding

The magnitude of what Christ did for us at Calvary defies description and is beyond understanding. No analysis can be satisfactorily conclusive. Our loftiest perception is always incapable of adequately defining God's intention and practice. There is a touch of infinity in all that He does.

He did not only die for our sin, He took our sin upon Himself. He was made sin for us. He spoke of our sin as if it was His own. He did not enjoy the humiliation. He endured the Cross and despised the shame. Everything He did for us was foreign to His nature. He had known nothing but love and pleasure in the presence of His Father, until His feet touched the ground. He was without sin and knew no sin. What a culture shock, if that was possible, to be confronted with a sinful world. No wonder He grieved and wept in the presence of sin.

Our understanding of God's design is limited by our flawed nature. We are the antitheses of all that He is. We are conceived in sin. We practice it, often with impunity. We have become familiar with it and many of its consequences. He, on the other hand, had an immaculate conception.

Predestined in the mind of eternity before the world began to be born of a virgin, sin, other than ours, had no part in His life. The love that led Him to do what He did was incomparable. It cannot be measured. It is like an ocean that has neither shore nor sea-bed.

Hound of Heaven

This Table represents the greatest, deepest, most comprehensive and profound expression of God's love. There is the ultimate and supreme abandonment here, for the essence of love is giving. There is real cost here—not tokens of appreciation, but blood, and sweat, and tears.

How can we possibly explain to others what love is, except we demonstrate it? Love contains both mystery and transparency. It is recognisable in its practice between husband and wife, mother and child, and between friends.

Separation and adverse circumstances serve to enrich it rather than deplete it. True love defies logic; it takes no offence. A mother's love is intensified for the rebellious member of the family. We weep over our own as He did over Jerusalem. We can escape from His judgement by the route of confession; we cannot escape from His love. That love is the weapon of the Hound of Heaven. "Even if I make my bed in hell—He is there."

His love for us was such that our distance and rebellion brought Him to the Cross. The Cross to us may be a place of shame with the stench of death about it, but because it was a measure of obedience, the Father, as He always does, sanctified it and heaven is now perfumed with the aroma of Golgotha.

There is a principle here: when we aim to please God, as He did, both heaven and earth are enriched.

Matthew 21:1–9

Pageantry To Passion

What a traumatic "Holy" week this was in the life of our Lord. At last the people believed that Jesus was what He claimed to be. They had just witnessed the most stunning of miracles in the raising of Lazarus from the dead. They were now ready to crown Him King in the 'Royal order of David'.

They had waited long for this. Not always patiently or peacefully. In the words of another, and in a different context, "our eyes have seen Thy salvation." So out came the palm branches and off came their garments, and down the hillside from the Mount of Olives to Jerusalem they triumphantly paraded their long expected King with the cries of "Hosanna to the Son of David" (Zechariah 9:9).

But like us, as so often we do, they completely misread the signs. I am not a King on a white charger riding to glory, I am a servant being led to my death.

Jesus was never impressed with pomp and ceremony. His mind was focussed on Calvary. There was a tree at the end of the road, but it wasn't a Palm tree! The crowd believed that the road from Olivet to Jerusalem with palm leaves was the road to glory, but all glory roads are strewn with blood and tears and sweat. Jerusalem to Calvary was the real glory road. Did He not say, "the hour is come when the Son of Man should be glorified"?! Those who cry "Hosanna" without understanding will also invariably cry "Crucify!" Those of us with an experience of the crucified Christ, spontaneously cry "Hosanna!"

Repentance

The Table is not primarily a place for good people. It has no ministry for such. It is for penitents who are aware of and hurt by their own sin. It is a place of cleansing and renewal rather than an award ceremony for the righteous. It is in the presence of the emblems that our sins rise up before us There is a cloud over us which inhibits our worship.

We are the cause of the table. Were it not for us, it would not be necessary. But, in the strange paradox of God's grace, it is not only our condemnation but our only hope of deliverance. David had sinned so grievously. Overcome by remorse and aware of the mercy of God in not cutting him off he cries, "Against Thee, Thee only, have I sinned." It was not the fear of God but the sense of hurt he had caused to a loving God that drove him to repentance, for it is the love of God which leads to repentance. We are always hurt by the hurt we cause to those whom we love. The more we love God and the closer we are to Him, the more difficult it is to sin, if for no other reason than that we don't want to hurt Him. We are the most comfortable in His presence when our conscience is clear.

It was Christ's declaration and expression of His love for Peter that prompted him to cry out, "Depart from me, for I am a sinful man." The Table demands repentance, and blessing depends on it. There is no forgiveness or cleansing without repentance.

Philippians 2:6–11

The ultimate humiliation

The Scriptures tell us "He humbled Himself". This self-inflicted act of humiliation did not begin at the Cross, nor even at Bethlehem. There is a sense of eternity about all the designs and activities of God. Humbled He was, in the perfect surroundings of Heaven. Slain from the foundation of the world.

The concept of a God in humiliation is beyond our understanding; a contradiction in terms. Our views of our personal humility and sometimes humiliation, are a pale shadow and on a different plane from that which brought our salvation. His coming into the world in humble circumstances and enduring a Cross of shame compounded the humiliation begun long since. In some ways it was not to death that He was obedient, but to the will of the His Father, and if that eventually meant death, so be it—indeed, He said so in the garden.

But, in some ways, it was in the manner of His death that He reached the rock-bottom of humiliation. The words "death on a Cross" were not just a description of how He died, to round off the story as it were. It is difficult for us after many years of Christian history, in which the Cross has been venerated as a sacred symbol, to understand the horror and disgust that this word provoked—it was an obscenity, a four letter word (CRUX). Even a strange formula was used rather than speak the word itself.

But like everything else that Heaven touches, when they nailed the Saviour there, He transformed it. The apostle confirms its credibility when he declares, "I will glory only in the Cross." It is a further confirmation of greatness. The lower we go, the higher we rise. The highest and best is reserved for those who are characterised by servanthood.

He had no need of repentance

Unlike us, the Saviour was never out of favour with God; never having to say sorry; having nothing to repent of. If a man is hungry he needs feeding. If a man is a sinner he needs saving. Awareness of our need is necessary if the need is to be met. We know from the experience of those who suffer from anorexia that they lose the sense of a need to eat. We also know that it can have fatal consequences. Unless we are aware of our need of a Saviour our sin continues to consume us and will, with certainty, prove eternally fatal.

In all God's plans for His people, the initiative has always been with Him—"while we were yet sinners Christ died for us." The Scriptures are lush with illustrations. But it is also true that the prerequisite in our salvation is with men—"Ye will not come to me that ye might have life." Like so much else when it comes to forgiveness there is both a positive and a negative. Like the wires in a plug, if one is detached there is no effect. All the power of positive salvation is with God and available in the work of the Saviour. It only becomes effective when the 'wire' of repentance is applied.

The whole credibility of the work of salvation rests on the perfection of the One who carried it out. The Lamb without blemish, untainted by sin; perfect in the sight of a Holy God and fully qualified for the work He came to do; the God-man in no need of repentance.

Millennium

We have recently celebrated the beginning of a Third Millennium. Remember the Millennium? How quickly we forget as one event is overtaken by another. Well, the fireworks and the other celebrations are soon gone, we are back to work and the 9 to 5 routine is soon restored. It can be as if it never happened.

All of life's pleasures and excitements are passing. Like the flower of the field and the dew of the morning, they are soon gone. Much of the pleasure in our lives is often not much more than a memory.

But those of us who have found faith and trust in God have entered into a marvellous inheritance. As we look for "a city not made with hands" so we look to a Millennium that is not bordered by time or even space. We belong to eternity. We share the nature of Him who had no beginning and has no end.

This Table has eternity written over it. On that fateful night before His journey to Calvary, He promised His disciples, and us, that He would again join us at another Table, when we would be invited to share, not in His sorrow, but in His glory.

When this wonderful Millennium, and possibly others after it, have gone, we look for one that has no end. The celebrations will be ongoing as we join with the angels in praising the One who has redeemed us. What a glorious endless day that will be! May we allow its anticipation to enrich the Table.

John 15:16

"Chosen"

"Ye have not chosen Me, I have chosen You". Why Me? Why us? you might well ask. I don't really know, do you ?

"He goeth unto a mountain and calleth whom He would". There was a crowd of people there but He didn't call them. There was no apparent reason for us to be called, nor for them, the crowd, not to be. Don't you see the wonder of His selective grace towards us ? "I will have mercy on whom I will" He declares. Whatever we may think of the justice of this arbitrary authority, it should cause us to marvel and wonder that of the many He should choose us. There is no logic or merit in His choice. We have less credit than many others. Few of us are rich, or particularly clever, and certainly not righteous.

"How unsearchable are His judgements." For some unknown reason—unknown to us, that is—He has set His love on us, and not others, and made us partakers of this very special feast. It should humble us, and thrill us, that we, of all people should find favour in His sight; we whose oft repeated and unrepentant sin is an affront to Hs purity.

We may not understand why He has chosen us from among many others but, with the undoubted privilege, He has put us under considerable obligation. There is a glorious sanctified self-interest in what He has done for us. Let's put the gift in context: "I have chosen you that you should bring forth fruit and that your fruit should remain."

Not just soul suffering

His suffering, like everything else He did, was complete. Our understanding and interpretation of truth is sometimes less than complete. What we say is true but contains less than all the truth.

Sometimes we say that, important as the physical suffering of the Saviour was, the real suffering was in His humiliation and isolation. But the two cannot be separated. They are two sides of the same coin: the reconciliation of heaven and earth; man made complete in God. He identifies with us in the sufferings of the body, and with the Father in His soul-suffering when made sin for us to fulfil God's justice.

The blood was real: the head crowned with thorns, the face smitten and spat upon, His back at the mercy of the oppressors. "See from His Head, His Hands, His Feet..." He was a Suffering Saviour in every sense of the term.

An old Greek Liturgy has the prayer, "Lord we beseech you by all the sufferings of Christ, known and unknown." This is an admirable summing up of the combined thrust of the work of the Cross. Part of it we can identify with, but there is much that belongs only to the mind of God.

Much of our own suffering is in consequence of our own sin, in many ways avoidable and self-imposed. We abuse our bodies, or at least fail to look after them properly. At times we wilfully make enemies of others who in turn cause us pain. But not so with Him; all His suffering was unsolicited and undeserved. Indeed, "this Man hath done nothing amiss."

Costly love

True love is always a costly thing. Love has always been a
driving force; it is a great motivator. The Scriptures and the
events of history are rich in their confirmation of this. Jacob
laboured without wages for seven years for the love of Rachael.
Jonathan surrendered the throne and bore the anger of his
father Saul for his love of David. Ruth abandoned her own
people for the love of Naomi. But great as these surrenders
were—and many more like them, and some no doubt greater—
they are understandable and their outcome predictable. The
costs were, to some extent, assessable.

But when we come to reflect upon what it cost for Christ to
express His love in the way that He did, we are really in a
different discussion or, as we say, in a "different ball-game". There
is a loss here we cannot quantify. How can we possibly
understand what it means to leave glory behind, with all the
worship and adoration of angels, to take on the restrictions of a
human body, to be acquainted with sorrows He had never known?
He was hungry and hurt, despised, rejected, betrayed by one of
His disciples and deserted by others. Then, hurt of all hurts, He
was abandoned by His Father to the ravages of hell itself.

We must have been in dire need of what He came to give if
such a cost was necessary. It was a cost that made enemies into
grateful friends. Although the cost to the Father through Jesus
the Son may forever remain a mystery to us, it does reflect the
value we are in God's sight.

Why Good Friday?

Here before us we have the emblems of that first Good Friday. Who on earth could ever have thought of calling it "good"?! It certainly wasn't the view of those who were there. At best it was just another day in the life of the soldiers, they had seen it all before. Although, having said that, their Commanding Officer was considerably distressed by it all. Although impressed by the dignity of the Man, he would not remember that day with any great pleasure. The disciples were just devastated—having thought that this was He who would restore Israel—others just hid themselves away. I rather think that if we had been there we would have joined them.

So why do we call it good? Hindsight is a wonderful thing. Subsequent events have helped to clear our vision and understanding. We are fortunate to live in post-resurrection times. Like many unpleasant experiences, the end often justifies and makes sense of the means. Nothing pleasant about the dentist's chair, but, my, the pleasure of relief when it brings a good night's sleep. Childbirth is every mother's Calvary—but there is joy in the morning with the first cry of new life.

All of us have our Good Friday experiences, some more serious that others. Our Resurrection may not come on the third day, or month or year, but come it will as surely as night follows day, if not in this world, then certainly in the next.

Some of our best Resurrections have followed our worst Good Fridays that we thought would never end. May we look for one in every trauma.

The inevitably of the Cross

If we allow for the kind of life that Jesus lived, it was well nigh inevitable that He would die as He did. He made many enemies in the short period of His preaching ministry. Although "the common people heard Him gladly", His message of spontaneity, freedom and inclusiveness, was in constant conflict with the religious pomposity of the Jewish leaders, and they were serious enemies to have. They were as determined to put Him to death as He was to die.

The Crucifixion was not an isolated act in His life. It was the climax of what He had long since begun. The giving God of the Old Testament was now the giving Christ of the new. There was a sense in which He was forever giving Himself, whether it was to a boy at the foot of a mountain, fearful disciples in a boat, a repentant, sinful woman at the well, a blind man on the road to Jerusalem, His weeping mother at the Cross, or the thief alongside Him. He was always sensitive and available.

It was ever God's intention to save His people from their own wilful destruction. The route was planned in eternity and executed in time. It was all "in the fullness of time". Had He come at another time, He might have been burnt at the stake or faced a firing squad. But the Cross, reaching as it were towards the skies, brought more than forgiveness of sin. It was an act of redemption, a means of restoration, placing us again under the canopy and protection of Heaven.

2 Peter 3:10

"I will come again"

It was, of course, Jesus who spoke these words and not Peter. Peter's up-beat confidence is written in a different context and with the benefit of some hindsight. In the resurrection he had witnessed Jesus "come back again" and that would confirm his belief that having done it once there was no reason to doubt it happening again.

Peter is trying to lift the spirits of his readers. When we wait, and wait, and wait for something or someone that never seems to come (you know the feeling), we can become discouraged and lose heart. The Master had promised to come back—but he hadn't. In some of His comments He had given the impression that it would be soon—"there are some standing here who shall not see death until I appear." Some were scoffing at this forlorn hope of the disciples. Peter is encouraging them to keep their faith and trust in the word of Jesus and ignore the scoffers. What God says He will surely do. How they ridiculed Noah for believing God, but how foolish they were as God kept His word. He always does, eventually. We live in an age when men are no less cynical. What an outrageous suggestion, they say, that God will return and call an end to the world as we know it.

'This old world has revolved on its axis since it evolved from its "big-bang birth" and we see no reason why it shouldn't continue to do so.' Peter says, how foolish are men of learning; slow to learn even from the events of history.

Why has He not come again?

Why? I don't know why. I confess I don't know and ask, Do you? Why hasn't He come, if coming He is? For the unbeliever, there is a tremendously frightening finality about the return of the Lord Jesus. In ignorance they fail to see this, but not so the Lord. No one knows better than He the awful consequences for the soul that is unprepared for His return—hence, in some measure, the delay in His coming.

"The Lord is not slack concerning His promises—but longsuffering." What a lovely word that is. Might it not be that His return to judgement is delayed by a compassion for the guilty? Any delay, if such be the case, is, ironically, to the benefit of the scoffer. An act of grace as God withholds His hand. But here, if I might suggest it, the long suffering is also an act of grace towards those of us who claim to be looking for His coming. Many of us are less than well-prepared for the event. The Apostle asks, in the light of His expected return, "what manner of men ought we to be in holy living and godliness."

The best preparation for His coming again is the practice of holy living: to grow in grace and in the knowledge of our Lord Jesus Christ. The suggestion is, that the more people that are brought into the kingdom and the more like Him we become, the sooner He will return. We influence His return by "hastening the day". The more we set our affection upon the Lord Jesus and find our pleasure in the things which gain His approval, the more we attain to His ambition for us "that we might be to the praise of His glory". He will tarry no longer when that happens to His people.

Isaiah 6:1–9

Gospel in the Old Testament

The Gospel according to St Matthew. How familiar. But the gospel according to Isaiah! Now that is something new. But why should it be? Because the Gospel is of God, it, like Him, has ever been. It was conceived in eternity past and will be consummated in eternity to come in a cascade of praise worthy of the Lamb that was slain.

It has always been God's intention to save His people. When He called to Adam in the Garden, it confirmed how anxious He was to restore the fellowship He always meant there to be. Estrangement offends and grieves Him. It is another measure of His love.

All the elements of the Table are exemplified in this gospel narrative. There is always the potential for blessing when we enter the place of worship. The sight of His glory causes our sin to surface and brings conviction and a sense of need. We are drawn into confession as we cry in penitence "woe is me". The seraphim Saviour touch brings cleansing to our soiled lives and, for once, we feel clean in His presence. Here is the gospel in drama as real and clear as anything in the New Testament, or since.

When the Scriptures tell us that "grace and truth came by Jesus Christ" this is not to suggest that, prior to the coming of the Saviour, these virtues were not already in existence, anymore than to suggest that the Holy Spirit was born at Pentecost.

These elements of the Gospel are as eternal as God Himself and belong as much to the Old Testament as the New.

When HE the Spirit is Come

"He will guide you into all truth." What an advantage we have over that company of first disciples who gathered around the table.

The witness of the Spirit within us adds confirmation to the work of the Cross. The grace of our Lord Jesus Christ in what He accomplished at Calvary, and the love of God which prompted it, may be beyond our understanding, but the illumination of the Holy Spirit made them credible and leads us into a greater understanding of the Table. We are different from others in our understanding when we have the Holy Spirit within us. His presence in our lives helps us to see the invisible and to feel the intangible. When the hymn-writer says, "I feel Thee mine," that is something that only the Spirit can communicate. While we may limit our interpretation of His presence in the elements, He is none the less real in His presence amongst us.

Communion, as we sometimes call the Table, is of course more than conversation. The NIV reads "fellowship", and what a lovely word that is. It is inclusive, suggesting a togetherness, a coming alongside each other, a sharing of the good and not so good experiences of our lives. Gathered as we are around the Table, the Communion takes on the added virtue of a re-union; kindred minds, borne along by that same Holy Spirit, as we pledge again our appreciation of all that the Saviour has done for us. We plight our troth and become one-again by the Spirit in the work of atonement.

As we are overpowered by the Spirit He empowers us in our understanding of His great work on our behalf.

Investing for eternity

The Cross was the greatest long term investment ever made. The lucrative dividends that have accrued from this single event are immeasurable. The "corn of wheat" has produced an income harvest greater than can be numbered; like the sand grains on the sea-shore or the stars in the heavens. An awareness of the eternal nature of any commitment can be a spur to making it. Because of the joy set before Him, the Saviour endured the Cross. He had an eternal mind-set that helped Him to see the end from the beginning. The light at the end of the tunnel at Golgatha was an empty tomb in the Garden, which itself was an earnest of a greater resurrection, the culmination of good seed well sown. Heaven is populated with His final dividend.

As with Him so with us. Notwithstanding the brevity of our time in the body, we are engaged in a long term investment plan. There is no quick fix in the establishment of the kingdom. If it took eternity before to prepare for Calvary, and eternity eventually to consummate it, we should be assured of the eternal nature of God's plan for us and our endeavour to serve Him.

Each day, as we sow or invest the good seeds in our words and actions and attitudes, it is so frustrating, disappointing and discouraging to see our witness rejected or ignored. We may be impatient to see some evidence that the seed has taken. If we know, and we do, that it happens in the ground, and indeed in the womb, why should we doubt it will happen in the heart? Unlike others with whom we are obliged to do business, His promise on our investments are gilt-edged and sealed in blood.

Inheritance

We often speak of our inheritance in Christ, and well we might. Everything He is and has is ours. To receive Christ is to receive all: "with Him, He gave us all things." The will and testament is signed and sealed in the blood of the New Testament as represented in the emblems of the Table.

But what of His inheritance in us? We speak and sing of all that we have in Him and for all that awaits us: our sins forgiven, our peace with God, our sense of His abiding presence by the Holy Spirit and the empowerment He gives us. We revel in the anticipation of an eternity spent in His immediate presence and all the perfect pleasure that will bring. But again I say, what of His inheritance in us? We see much in Him that causes us to treasure our inheritance in Him, but what does He see in us that brings a smile of approval? Paul says in his letter to the Ephesians that we can add to His pleasure by adding to His inheritance in us lives that are lived to His glory. It is to His Glory when He sees the evidence of His work in us.

The same power which helped Him to die is available to help us to live: to live our lives in victory over the things that spoil our lives and to build holiness which will provide an inheritance for Him in which He will be well pleased. When the Apostle Paul speaks of power he dwells on superlatives because he himself found God superlative. Power to the Apostle is "exceeding great"; there is more than enough to defeat temptation, to break sinful habits and to live above our circumstances. Just what He is looking for as an inheritance in us.

Hopeless condition

When it comes to the spiritual dimension in our lives, if there is one thing that is obvious it is that we do not have the capacity to pick ourselves up "by the shoelaces". Our experience confirms our weakness; the good that we would, we do not and the evil that we would not, that we do. The Bible uses vivid language to describe our condition: "without strength," "Christ died for the ungodly," "dead in trespasses and sins," "while we yet sinners." Weak, ungodly, dead, sinners—strong words indeed.

Sinners—short of the standard, missing the mark that God has set for those who lay claim to pleasing Him. Loving Him with all our heart, mind and soul? Regrettably it cannot be, for all have sinned and come short of His glory.

Ungodly—maybe we are sinners, but we were born that way and it is not of our own making or responsibility. But ungodly is more than a condition, it is a wilful deliberate act of continuous rebellion towards God and His plan for our lives.

Weak—like the man who is waist-deep in quicksand, the more we struggle the deeper we sink. Arms pinned to our side, feet locked in mud, any help must come from someone other than ourselves. Held fast in the quicksand of sin—not only born into it, but now living in it—we are powerless to extract ourselves.

Dead—can't be much more hopeless than that. No sensitivity or response to spiritual influences that forever surround us. When it comes to a relationship with God, little wonder we are described as dead.

Any hope in our hopelessness can only be found in the love that God has for us and has shown to us. Whatever our condition or circumstances there is always a "but". "But God, who is rich in mercy...", can give life to dead men and woman, and deliverance from the guilt and the power of sin and death.

Beyond the Cross

If someone is in the midst of great trauma and personal grief it is difficult, and sometimes insensitive, to suggest to them that they should look beyond their current circumstances towards the future and the bigger picture. Often, to such, there is no tomorrow or, if there is, it is no more than an extension of the present and they would rather not think about it.

In this respect the Saviour had an advantage over His friends on that last dreadful evening He spent with them. Being who He was, He knew that His tomorrow was going to be better. The disciples, saddened and devastated with the news that He was going to leave them, felt not even hope for the future, to say nothing of the assurance that He had that all would ultimately be well.

Those of us who live knowing the consequences of Calvary, have the advantage on these early followers. The resurrection has begotten a hope within us that, for the believer, death can never be final. Created as we are in the image of God, and re-created from a nature flawed by sin, we are made for eternity. He wants us to share in the assurance that He had, that every cross we bear is a preparation for the glory He intends to share with us. It was so for Him with the Father, it will be so for us. We look upon the experience of death as the means by which we enter into that glory and the more immediate presence of the Lord, and it might well so happen. But contrary to the common belief that death is a certainty for all, the truth is otherwise. The Word of God exhorts us not to look for death, but for the more pleasant and exhilarating experience of His return.

Incomplete as yet

Although the cross is referred to us as 'the finished work of Christ'—"it is finished"—it was in its way, and in a sense, more a means to an end, a contribution towards God's plan for His people. The end game was that sinful men would be reconciled to God; the tranquillity of Eden would be restored; communion unsullied by sin—not just the absence of evil, but the companionship of God walking in the new garden. God and man together again in perfect harmony as always was His intention. To that end the Cross was necessary. It required an atonement—an at-one-again to bridge the gap between God and man.

Again, in a sense, God's overall plan was conceived in eternity past and awaits eternity to come for its final consummation. The Cross is pivotal and is a linchpin which makes possible our reconciliation to God on the strength of our confession and adherence. Saved we are, sanctified almost we may be. But there is more to our salvation than that. God's ambition for us is always beyond our own, indeed, beyond our understanding. The Apostle tells us with mouth-watering enthusiasm that the eye can't see nor the tongue tell what marvellous things God has prepared for us. He loves us so much. With all our weakness, and don't we know it, we are perfect now in His sight, as one day we will be in our own. Even more wonderful, we shall be perfect as He is now. The significance of the Cross is in its consequences for the future. Even those who have gone before cannot be "made perfect" until we join them. Another paradox, maybe, with Him yet unfulfilled until the family is complete. Even so Lord, come quickly.

"A light to the Gentiles"

The best possible news for those of us who were not really His people. It was always His intention that, beginning at "Jerusalem", His kingdom would have no boundaries. He came unto His own and they—for the most part—did not accept Him, but to as many—of His own people—who did receive Him, He made especially His own. It is of great consolation that in every recorded rebellious people there has been a faithful remnant.

All light has its origin in God; it is of the essence of His nature. The Apostle John in his first epistle declares that God is Light (1:5). Not that He possesses light, or even sheds light (both of which are true), but that He is Light. Light brings revelation. It reveals what is already there but not seen. The room that appeared reasonably clean in the evening is shown for what it is in the clear light of day. The 'white' ceiling is now cream. God did not primarily become man that He might befriend us or share our sorrows, but as a Light to reveal God in a world where sin had obscured Him. The result of revealing God is an awareness of our need of Him as a Saviour, as we feel uncomfortable in His presence. Darkness does not sit easily with light; they are incompatible. I am told that the introduction of gas was more responsible than any law for the reduction in crime.

He is always the Light at the end of our personal tunnel of darkness. This Table for all men is one way He chose to demonstrate it. As Gentiles and foreigners we are forever grateful to this all-inclusive Saviour.

The Jireh God

The message of the Table is the ultimate provision by a God who has been forever giving. It was a beautiful garden in a perfect environment for our first parents. It was a supply of lifesaving "corn in Egypt" for Jacob's sons; a reluctant deliverer when He chose Moses to lead His people into freedom, and manna in the wilderness for the disobedient children of Israel. It was an unfailing cruse of oil for the prophet and those who befriended him. Thousands on the hillside were more than satisfied, not with the boy's lunch, but what the Saviour did with it. If the sparrow in the air and the flower of the field are the declared object of His provision, how much more are we, created as we are in His image and redeemed at such a cost?

There is a constant stream of Divine intervention throughout the Biblical history of God's people, and others, to make provision of all kinds where there is a need. None of this should really surprise those of us who have any knowledge or experience of parenting. We do it, not because it is a general principle of species that we care for those we have begotten, or because we feel obliged to provide for our own as part of our responsibility, but we do it primarily because we love them and want to.

The worldling takes God's provision for granted, often unaware that He is the provider. When the lines fall in pleasant places self-made man considers it to be either a reward for his endeavour or a stroke of good fortune.

I trust we know better. The Table represents the most conclusive evidence of the provision that God has made for the deepest of all our needs.

"I call you friends"

We all need friends. We were not meant to make our own way in life; we never were. We are not that kind of creature. We may not hunt in packs, but we do value and thrive on company. God Himself recognised that when He created our first parents for each other. Even He exists in a threesome.

If it is true that we need friends, I think it is even more true that each of us needs at least one special friend, one to whom we can open our heart and share our deepest feelings in the sure knowledge that it will not become the subject of idle gossip.

The writer of Proverbs acknowledged this when he stated that "there is a Friend that sticketh closer than a brother". Everything a good friend can be to us and do for us, the Saviour can be and do better.

He is the most caring of all our friends. He feels for us in a way that is more than being sorry for us. It means that when we try to do the right thing and fail, He does not criticise us as some of our friends might do, but sympathises with our failure because He understands our weakness. We cast our care upon Him for He cares for us. The more we share the company of our family and friends, the more we understand each other. And the more we keep close company with the Lord the more we experience His sympathetic friendship and understanding.

He is so faithful. We may, and do, fail Him; but He never. His friendship is classically shown in what He did for us at Calvary, suffering for us, accepting the punishment for our sin, laying down His life for His friends, among whom we are numbered.

What a Friend we have in Jesus!

He is Risen

The Resurrection makes sense of every perceived tragedy in the earthly life of our Lord. What a difference it would have made to the disciples that awful night of foreboding if they had been assured of the Resurrection. Notwithstanding the promises He had made from time to time such an event would have been considered inconceivable. In this day of grace we are privileged to look beyond the Table to an empty garden tomb.

If the Cross was inevitable because of the confrontation of His life with the pride of men, so too was His rising from the dead. If His death had to have any effective meaning, it had to be followed by Resurrection. What value has a seed that is sown if it remains dead in the ground. The Resurrection was as much part of the Atonement as was the Cross. It was the Father's seal of approval on what the Son had accomplished. "Him hath God raised from the dead." Only a living Lord could be a living foundation for the Church He had promised to establish.

What a marvellous day to celebrate this most glorious of events! That first Easter Day the Lord of life defied all the laws of nature except His own to establish a new life for all who would follow in His train. "Because I live, you shall live also" is the guarantee of our eternity. Sealed by His shed blood and compounded in the dust of an empty tomb. This is a Table whose solemnity is wreathed in glory. Our participation at the Table is a foretaste of what awaits us. We have His word: "Father, that they might share in the glory which we had before the world began."

"That they may be one—as We are"

The Lord's ambition for us is always of the highest. He does set the most challenging demands upon us. Whatever does He mean by this? That our unifying relationships with each other should be as His is with the Father? Incredible surely, if not well nigh impossible! He was so much at one with the Father that everything He said and did was in perfect harmony with the Father's will. How could we possibly aspire to such a relationship with our fellow believers? Surely our flawed nature would prohibit such a practice of our faith.

With all the limitations we have to measure up to His demands, it can be an exciting adventure to pursue the goal of a fellowship with each other that bears the hallmark of the unity that exists between the Father and the Son. Our unity with each other will be determined by the measure of our unity with the Father in His will for our lives. "I do always the thing that pleases the Father," says Jesus thus endorsing the unity that they enjoyed. His perfect understanding of the Father's will was the clue to their unity. "I and the Father are one."

This is our role model. We cultivate an understanding of our fellow believers with all our differences in personality and approach; we bear and forbear with each other and invoke the help of the Holy Spirit as we fellowship together in tolerance of the views of each.

As we share with the Father, He encourages us to find in Him the resources to help us in bringing unity to the fellowship. The differences in our temperament and background can be overcome in the unity of the Spirit.

Ever-present Saviour

If Jesus Christ be God Incarnate, then all the glorious attributes
of the Father dwell fully in Him. His all-seeing and all-knowing
(Omniscience) characteristic begets an always-present-
everywhere (Omnipresence). In a sense, there is no past,
present and future with Him. He is an unchanging Man for All
Seasons and for every age and circumstance. He is as present
with one person as with another, and in any one of all places
simultaneously. Knowing all there is to know about us, He is
present in every circumstance of our life—encouragingly,
everywhere at the same time. No matter where we have been,
or are, or ever will be, He is there. We just cannot get away
from His presence. "In the womb before we were born," the
Psalmist declares His presence to be. Locations mean nothing
to Him. "Whither shall I go from thy Spirit?" God is a Spirit,
unconfined by space, who recognises no borders. It is not so
much that He accompanies us, or follows us, rather it is that
wherever we are, He is already there: "I go before you." It is as
if He anticipates our movements.

As with distance, so it is with circumstance: He is always
present. When at the end of our tether in our most difficult of
circumstances, we can be sure He will be there. Even in the
darkness of our frustrations and disappointments, our
assurance of His presence will lighten the gloom. In our most
sinking experiences we are kept afloat by His continuing
presence.

That presence can be as real to us, if not more so, as it was
to those who were with Him around the Table in the Upper
Room.

The Supremacy of Christ

The Apostle is at his most exhilarating when he speaks or writes about the Saviour. You can sense his excitement as he eulogises over the Lord Jesus in his letter to the church at Colosse. He seems almost to run out of superlatives in his exultation of his superlative Saviour. He is everything we are not. In all that was ever of importance, He has no peer. All other pedestals and their idols collapse when He is present. He wears His crown without challenge.

He is incomparable. Eternity is His name; for as long as God has been around, so has He. Some of us may be considered the image of our father, He was the "express image" of His. The prophets were describing Him long before He was born. In their eulogies, they were as ecstatic as the Apostle: "Wonderful, Counsellor, Mighty God, Prince of Peace," "King of Kings," "Saviour," "Immanuel," and so it goes on. He had need of nothing. "All that the Father hath is Mine."

The Apostle was for ever praising the exceeding abundance of the grace that not only saved him, but had fitted him for such a proud office. He claims that the riches of Christ are "unsearchable". Not that they can't be found, but rather that they can't be fathomed. Christ is supreme in everything He is and does for us. Because His wealth is infinite we have no standard by which to measure it. We may describe His grace as rich, or very rich, as even embarrassingly rich, but there is no descriptive adjective that can adequately do justice to the supremacy of His greatness in the hierarchy of Heaven.

When He is supreme in our thinking and in the practice of our daily lives, we are equipped by the Spirit with a godliness that welcomes every opportunity to meet around His Table.

Reservoir of Power

Only One with the power to change the outcome could see the death of an only Son as a declaration of victory. A power borne out of a confidence in His ability to crown such death with Resurrection. God is Omnipotent; everything is within His power. He can do anything He chooses to do. He may 'allow' the unprofitable to happen, but everything He 'does' is with profit. Asks the cynic, "Can God make a rock He cannot lift?" Men may say and do foolish and ridiculous things, but never God. They seek the spectacular for its own virtue; God does nothing that is out of character. Every expression of His power is consistent with who and what He is. He is not only the Creator but the Sustainer of all that is good. The Psalmist says that "the heavens declare the glory of God and the firmament His handiwork". "Such knowledge is too wonderful for me," adds the writer, and it certainly is for all of us. My learned friends tell me that if I could travel at the speed of light, it would be 2 million years before I arrived at some of the stars! And, wonder of wonders, its your God and mine who holds all this in the palm of His hand.

Again, as with much else, even His power and sovereignty are personalised. He holds in reserve all that is necessary to sustain all that He has created. Equally, that same power which has re-created us, has all that is needed to keep our spirits alive. We may not know what a day may bring forth, but He does. He is never taken unawares by what happens to us and has already insured against all that might happen to us. What a sense of serenity it brings to know that this God of all power has us constantly on His mind and heart.

"How precious also are Thy thoughts towards me."

"Go————————make Disciples"

In the strange economy of God's plan, He has chosen to condition much of it on our willingness to co-operate with Him in implementing it. Sovereign and Omnipotent as He is, He still doesn't expect them "to hear without a preacher". Or, like the impotent who claimed there was "no man to put him into the pool," Jesus said, "As the Father hath sent Me, even so I send you." Focus on the "as" and "even so". Sent by the Father, He was commissioned, ordained, and equipped to redeem and reconcile. "Even so send I you."

There is no greater imperative in Scripture than to evangelise. It is not only clearly defined but expressed explicitly as a command. When the Word says, "Go," we ignore it at our peril. There is a legitimacy about outreach that is not exclusively dependent upon faith. Wesley said, "We evangelise or perish," and he would have been a nine day wonder if he hadn't practised his own precept. Every businessman knows the value, if not the necessity, of investment and growth. We need make no apology for a principle well established in the secular world. The commission of those of us who have had a transforming encounter with Christ, has always been to "go forth and tell". No one has a legal liberty to pursue an interest which would injure society, and by the same token we have no moral liberty to withhold the means of saving that same society. Those of us who remain passive spectators of the misery caused to our family, friends and others, by sin, while we are in possession of the means of relieving it, are guilty by default.

Passion for Him will itself prompt within us a passion for others.

Forgiveness through repentance

There is a principle of supply and demand in the realm of forgiveness. The demand is universal and complete for all have sinned; the supply is inexhaustible and readily available for its source is in God. The reconciliation of the two is inhibited only by our unwillingness to make confession. The resolve to forgive is born out of our own experience of forgiveness; as a forgiven people we are obliged to forgive, it is not an option. Its effectiveness, however, is dependent on the confession of the guilty, as was the case in our conversion. The object of forgiveness is reconciliation and requires a willingness to be reconciled. To forgive without confession is an affront to God's judgement, and tantamount to condoning the offence. Repentance is a prerequisite to forgiveness.

The Word of God leaves us in no doubt about the essential relationship between repentance and forgiveness. They are two sides of the same coin, and like any coin are only valid when both are embossed. In all His dealings with sinful men and women, even when repentance is not explicitly expressed, it is implicit in action. The act of repentance by the woman in the Pharisee's house brought a word of cleansing from the Lord. It was so with the feeble words of the dying thief; indeed, we refer to him as the "penitent thief". The faith that brings forgiveness is more than the spoken word of confession, and often expresses itself in thought and actions which the Lord recognises as coming from a "broken and a contrite heart". He delights to speak the peace of forgiveness to such. The Word of God sets very high standards for us as we practise forgiveness, indeed, well nigh impossible one might say. But there is always grace available to help us measure up. He is gracious in our weakness. He does not pass judgement on our failed attempts to succeed, but He does regret our miserly efforts, and sometimes failure even to try.

"If only———"

If we could only choreograph the direction of our own lives, how different and much more attractive the pageantry would be. The elimination of everything that disables us would enhance our quality of life. But, as we know, life is just not like that. It wasn't for the greatest of all examples and role models; why should it be otherwise for His creation? Even for our Saviour there came a time in the Garden when His desire was for some other way to achieve the same end and thus avoid the Cross.

Life is a rich tapestry but many of its stiches are not as we would have planned. All life's colours are not dull; neither are they all glowing red. At times we drink from the bitter waters of Marah; at other times the champagne of joy brings its happiness as we hear the cry of the new-born baby.

Why do we sometimes question the negatives of our circumstances but, seemingly, never the good things that come our way? We receive the dreaded words from the consultant which we had hoped we would never hear. "Why me Lord?" we might be tempted to ask, "What about all the bad people, Lord?"

It's a line we seldom take when we are reflecting on God's goodness. I sometimes look at the Table and wonder, "Why me Lord? What about all the good people out there who are more deserving than I am?" We are not called upon to ignore circumstances, but to look through them and beyond them to a glorious end, which more than justifies every perceived adverse circumstance. When Jesus prayed for a possible alternative way to fulfil His commission, the Father did not view it as a wavering doubt, but as a prelude to an amazing submission to His will. When doubts assail us and circumstances cast a shadow over our decisions, then the "never-the-less" of the Garden can lead us into peace.

Mark 16:3

Who will roll away the stone? (1)

There was no animation amongst the women that morning, no spring in the step. This was no Palm Sunday. What about the stone? Maybe they should have asked some of the men to come with them, if they could have found them. Peter would have been the obvious choice, but he had been sulking since Friday. Perhaps the soldiers will help; that kind Centurion might be there. Of course it would have been different if they had asked us? Based on our three-year experience of His miraculous ministry we would have known that the stone would be rolled away! The arrogance of hindsight is worse than the doubt and unbelief of the present.

One of Timothy Dudley Smith's hymns speaks of focussing, not on what was accomplished even, but rather on Him. However, in the context of this incident there are lessons we might learn from those who are in the frame. The women, for example: I know little of biology or psychology but I wonder if in some, if not many, respects we men are the "weaker sex"! I do not wish to appear patronising—if for no other reason than I would fear the consequences!—but there is a sensitivity here that I envy and it reflects that of the MASTER. There is a intuitive spontaneity about their action. There is no record of questions being asked. How could we possibly go? ...the stone will be there and the soldiers! Incidentally, as far as we can see, the men had no intention of going.

What a lovely story of uninhibited love. It could well be that they had been on such earlier missions of charity for family and friends whom they had lost, but somehow the intensity of this was different. The glorious outcome was to be different too.

Mark 16:3

Who will roll away the stone? (2)

Such is the abounding, transcendent, incomprehensible love of the Father towards those of us who are peculiarly His own, that He appears to work on our behalf even when our faith is less than quantifiable. When our gloom is such that our faith is submerged, He sympathises with our weaknesses and recalls His own agony of soul in the Garden. He applies His grace upon grace, and envelopes us in His love. He refuses to allow the gloom to shut out His presence

As He did with these marvellous women, so with those of us who are looking for Him. For them the grass was greener on the other side of Calvary. The Risen Lord who declared, "Behold I go before you into Galilee" was echoing the promise, "Behold I go before you to make the crooked paths straight." The last thing on the minds of the women was that they might find an empty tomb. Theirs was a simple, almost a mundane act, of affection, but unknown to them they were making a journey into history. Posterity records their experience and they share their hosannas with us. Simply by going to the tomb they put themselves in the way of unanticipated blessing, and what a reward they had for their endeavour!

What an encouraging re-assurance there is for those of us who are fearful of what difficulties await us. As we walk the walk of faith, as we are obliged to do, we wonder at times what lies beyond the hill and hidden from our sight. Is the climb worth making? Will the effort bring further frustration and disappointment? O for a man to move the stone! For all who walk by faith there is always a Man to do just that. It is of His nature to make a way for His people. As a "rewarder of those who diligently seek Him"—in a way the women were doing—He is never a disappointment and can transform our desolation with the joy of His appearing.

Greatest Thing in the World

The attributes of God are incomparable—not only in the quality, but in degree—which makes it difficult to speak or write of them with any feeling of having done them justice. Every virtue we possess or can ever possess, is held in perfection in the nature of God.

If light, as some say is the most comprehensive of all God's attributes, then love must surely be the most sublime and understandable. All God's activity is borne of love. That is why it is the greatest. The world would be a much poorer place without love. Its practice cancels out much of the evil around us. All love has its origin in God. God not only shows His love, He bestows it. It is not acquired by any natural means, but like everything from God, it is a gift.

Real love expresses itself in many ways, as we know from our own human experience. Its characteristics of unselfishness contrasts boldly with the acquisitive self-seeking practices of society. As the Bible puts it, "love does not seek its own." Paul speaks of the Lord Jesus "emptying Himself". Love always concedes; it does not insist on its 'rights', no matter how legitimate they may be. Every real relationship depends upon this principle of giving way to another.

We are the product of His living and dying love, and we please Him best as we practise it in our dealings with others. It is often so difficult to consider our own reputation of no real value when that of others is at stake. He did, so again we find His smile of approval as we try. This eventually put Him on the Cross. He asks us to carry our cross every day with pride.

A Righteous Man to Die

The magnitude of the Cross is startling in its mystery, significance, and implication. There is no legitimacy in a cross-death where the law has not been broken. To make the Cross effective in our salvation it required a "righteous" man to be made sin, while at the same time remaining the righteous Son of God. While the great Apostle often staggers in amazement at what is happening here, I make no apology for my lack of understanding. Nevertheless, righteous He is, and ever was. God is, above all others, righteous. Everything He does is right. His promises are foolproof; His word is His bond, and His integrity beyond question. He is all that we would want in a best friend, completely reliable and incapable of betrayal or deceit. We are attracted to such a person. We fall in love with such, and pledge ourselves in response.

If we were to cultivate such qualities of transparency maybe others would be similarly attracted. Our witness through lives of integrity, which is right and proper in itself, may also be a means to a good end in leading others into faith. We may find difficulty with some of God's attributes for one reason or another, but surely here is one to which we can apply ourselves: to be known amongst our friends and others as one who can be trusted; dependable and a defender of those who slip and fall and fail. The Centurion was impressed with the Righteous Man on the Cross. We are called to reflect Him as we live before others.

Such a redeemed lifestyle brings a smile to the face of Heaven and the lifestyle that brings the approval of Heaven will be rewarded with peace and contentment and a sense of fulfilment. It will enrich our own lives and that of others.

The Cross—its Transforming Continuity

If it is God's intention that we should be "conformed to the image of His Son", then something very radical has to be done with us and to us. If we are to be like Him we must appreciate the mountain we are asked to climb. We are so badly flawed by sin that only a cross with its cleansing and renewal properties could make the necessary difference. We are sinners, not only in part, but "altogether gone astray". On the other hand, He operates from a base of perfection: everything that He is, is what He always was. All our tendencies are towards rebellion against God, His always towards reconciliation. He is so infinitely different from us. All His virtues are inherent and spontaneously displayed; any we have are gifted and require discipline and positive action to express them. How on earth can we be expected to reach such impossible standards?

In the light of this seemingly impossible dream and depressing assignment, I am glad the Cross is so comprehensive and inclusive in what it has accomplished. It meets every need of the past, present and future. It has cancelled my sin and equipped me by the Holy Spirit to overcome its power in my life. One day He will release me from its very presence. All this should be no surprise, for everything He does He performs to perfection.

All the efficacy of the Cross and His Resurrection is carried into His continuing work on our behalf. He knows and cares for us in our limitations and need. He is so gracious. He honours our commitment to holy living, even though the presence of sin may leave us less than satisfied with our progress towards His likeness.

New life through the Cross

In the often strange paradox of logic, all life has its origin in death. "Except a corn of wheat fall into the ground and die, it cannot come alive." In that context it is not particularly surprising that Christ should rise up from the dead. As He himself said, it is necessary for one Man to die to take sin and bury it in the bowels of hell where it belongs. It has no lasting place in the kingdom and economy of God. His rising brought new life that was more consistent with God's intention for all His creation.

That is something of how much we owe to Christ's death. It spawned a life that has no end. He Himself is Life itself and has begotten us in a lively hope. He has put eternity in our soul and made us as deathless as He is. John says that his gospel was written "that you might have life" and again, in his Epistle "that you might know that you have eternal life". The life He gives is His life. It is a resurrection life and we know what that did for the disciples! Amongst other things, it brought daybreak to the gloom of Good Friday. They may not have fully understood it but they were elated. It is not a presumption to believe that we are the possessors of this new life from God, but rather is it offensive to God to doubt it when He has so clearly declared it to be so. "Whosoever has the Son has life," insists the same Apostle with embarrassing regularity. As we surrender to the discipline of the Cross, He will raise us up in a continuing experience of new life and make us a testimony to others.

Need to be reminded

This Table of Remembrance is also eloquent evidence of our need to be reminded. This is not merely a request to remember Him, but a command to acknowledge Him. It is not only a place of thanksgiving but also of repentance. It is a recognition of the goodness of God that leads us into the way of repentance, and where better to find it than here. As we reflect upon what God has done for us and, hopefully, in us and through us, our sense of unworthiness brings us into penitence.

The book of Deuteronomy, which I don't suppose many of us use in our daily devotions, is a catalogue of constant reminders and repetitions of all that has been said already. How these early people of God needed to be reminded of what God had said and done, and of their negative, or at best lack of, response to His goodness. And don't we all need to be reminded of the same goodness? Remember what Paul wrote to the Philippian church: "to write the same things, to me is not grievous, but for you is safe."

We need to hear what God is saying and doing, not once but many times over. And so it was with this rebellious people. Moses says, "I have told you before and tell you again..." Memory is often our Achilles heel; we remember things we should forget, and forget those we should remember. The evidence for the goodness of God is so overwhelming that any average lawyer would rest his case in minutes with complete confidence in the outcome. This Table should flow with repentance as we call to mind His goodness. In the paradox of blessing, as we hang our head in shame, it will strangely warm our hearts.

The Cross—God's anger

The Cross is a demonstration of God's anger against sin, as well as of love for the sinner. It is an awful thing to fall into the hands of an angry God. Sin discovered that on Golgotha's hill to its eternal cost. It was there He destroyed the power of sin and its consequences of death and hell.

In any judgements we are tempted to make, we must never exclude God's anger. It is as much a part of His character as is His more attractive love. It was not only His love for us that put Him on the Cross, but also His intense hatred of sin itself. His judgements are never overruled by His love; they are complementary, essential to each other. They are parallel twin rails which keep God's purposes on track and credible. When we love someone dearly, we hate everything that would hurt them.

When God declares of His ancient people in the wilderness that "not a man of this evil generation shall see (much less enter) the land", He is obviously displeased. What judgement! But see the grace in the exemption of Caleb and Joshua, both acknowledged for their well- documented stand for faith, trust and confidence.

The Man on the Cross has taken the full brunt of God's anger with sin, and those of us who, on our confession, have been "accepted" by Him are "excepted" from His judgement. However, the believer in disobedience is not free from God's disapproval. The unconfessed and sometimes wilful sin brings confusion to our relationship with the Father, and can condemn us to a wilderness experience which was never God's intention for us.

I am glad that God is angry, for I know that His anger is directed only against everything that hurts. He is angry with my sin because He knows better than I what it is doing to me. Anything that makes God angry should make me angry too.